Repentance and Faith

REPENTANCE AND FAITH

EXPLAINED TO THE UNDERSTANDING
OF THE YOUNG

CHARLES WALKER

SOLID GROUND CHRISTIAN BOOKS
BIRMINGHAM, ALABAMA, USA

Solid Ground Christian Books
2090 Columbiana Rd, Suite 2000
Birmingham, AL 35216
205-443-0311
sgcb@charter.net
http://solid-ground-books.com

Repentance Explained to the Understanding of the Young
Faith Explained to the Understanding of the Young

Charles Walker (1791-1870)

Both *Repentance & Faith* were originally published by
The American Tract Society

Solid Ground Classic Reprints

First printing of new edition April 2006

Cover work by Borgo Design, Tuscaloosa, AL
Contact them at nelbrown@comcast.net

Cover image is taken from the frontispiece of REPENTANCE,
EXPLAINED TO THE UNDERSTANDING OF THE YOUNG, *and is taken
from the picture of False Repentance found in chapter two, pp. 18-26.*

ISBN: 1-59925-064-0

REPENTANCE

EXPLAINED TO THE UNDERSTANDING
OF THE YOUNG

CHARLES WALKER

PREFACE

THE writer of this little work has long been convinced that many of the professedly religious books put into the hands of children are, at best, of an equivocal character, containing but very little sound moral instruction in the midst of masses of romance ; and that not a few of them exert a positively bad influence on the taste, habits, and morals of the children and youth of our land. He has often been sad, while reflecting that even the libraries of our Sabbath-schools, formed avowedly for the purpose of instructing the young in the things of religion, and of saving their souls, contain such a number of works tending to create an appetite for novel-reading, and to form a taste which will turn away with disgust from the sober discussions of religious truth.

To justify this immense amount of mere story-telling and fiction, it is said that books, to engage the attention of the young, must be interesting, and that the narrative form of giving instruction is most attractive to youthful minds. This is true. But does it follow that every family and Sabbath-school library in the land must be flooded with religious novels ? May not the narrative form of giving instruction be, in a great measure, retained without this ?

For the purpose of illustration, the writer sees no valid objection to the introduction of a short supposed case, as in the parable of Nathan to David, and in those of the Saviour; but to construct a book of fiction on the plan of a novel, having the needful plot and development, and which will be read for the interest which the story excites, and to call it a religious book, and put it into the hands of children and youth for the purpose of making them pious, is, in the writer's apprehension, like sending them to the theatre to promote their morals. In either case they might hear or read many good things, but these good things are so mingled with trash, or neutralized by romantic excitement, as to be productive of little benefit and much harm.

Another prominent fault in books designed for children is, that many of them are written in a style wholly foreign from their modes of expression, and altogether above their comprehension. If it were not too serious a matter, it would be really laughable to notice the uncommon and pompous words, the stately and high-sounding phraseology of many books written professedly for children and for Sabbath-school libraries.

The writer of the following little work has attempted to discuss an important doctrine of the Gospel, and to urge its correspondent duty on the conscience of the reader. And he has attempted to do this in language which children may understand, and in a form which may excite their attention. How he has succeeded in the attempt the Christian public must judge. To them, and to the blessing of the Saviour, he cheerfully, but with much diffidence, commends it.

CONTENTS

CHAPTER I.

SUBJECT OF THE BOOK—EXPLANATION OF REPENTANCE.

CHAPTER II.

FIRST STORY—FALSE REPENTANCE.

CHAPTER III.

SECOND STORY—TRUE REPENTANCE.

CHAPTER IV.

BIBLE EXAMPLES—PETER.

CHAPTER V.

DAVID'S REPENTANCE.

CHAPTER VI.

THE PRODIGAL SON.

REPENTANCE

CHAPTER I.

My young Reader—This little book is on the subject of *repentance*. I want you should read every word of it. I want you to think about it as you read, and see if you understand it. Some young persons do not try much to understand what they read. They just look over the leaves of a book in a careless manner, and think nothing about it afterwards. Now I hope that those who take this book will not be so careless. I hope that every one of my young readers will read this book through, read it carefully, think about what is said in it, and get good from it.

I am going to tell you what repentance is, and how good people feel and do when they repent. You know that God commands us to repent. The Holy Bible speaks often of the duty of repenting. When John the Baptist began to preach, he said, "Repent ye, for the kingdom of heaven is at hand." He meant, that the Saviour was coming to set up his kingdom in the world, and that men ought to leave off their wicked doings, and live holy lives. When Jesus came, he began to preach in the same way. "From that time Jesus began to preach, and to say, Repent, for the kingdom of heaven is at hand." Matt. 4 : 17. He meant, that he was come to set up a church in the world, and that men should give up their wicked feelings and habits, and that they should become pious, so that they might belong to his church, which is his kingdom on earth. The apostles also preached repentance. "And they went out, and preached that men should repent." Mark 6 : 12. And in the great city of Athens, as Paul was speaking to the people, he said, "God now commandeth all men every where to repent."

Thus you see that God says that all men should repent. And why should all men repent? Because they are sinners. They have done wrong. They have had wicked thoughts and feelings. They have spoken wicked words.

They have done wicked things. And besides, they have not done what God told them to do. They have not obeyed the commands of God given in the Bible. They have not minded what Jesus Christ said about " loving God with all their hearts, and their neighbors as themselves." It is for these things that God commands all men to repent. And must young persons and children repent? Yes, they are sinners. God means them when he says that all should repent. Every little boy and girl who reads this book is a sinner. You have done wrong a thousand times. You have had wicked feelings. Perhaps you have been angry, and have told lies. You have disobeyed your parents, and have not loved God, and prayed to him, and served him as you ought to have done. You are therefore a sinner, and God says you must repent.

You can never be saved without repentance. God has provided a way to save sinners. He sent his only begotten Son to deliver us from sin, and from " the wrath to come." Jesus Christ, the Son of God, came into our world, and suffered and died to redeem us. By his sufferings and death he made an atonement "for our sins, and not for ours only, but also for the sins of the whole world." But all this will not profit you, unless you embrace this way of salvation, and become a friend and follower of Jesus Christ. You will never be saved, unless you come to Jesus as the Saviour; and you will never come to Jesus unless by repentance. You must see and feel that you are a guilty sinner; and then you must cast yourself on his mercy, and rely on what he has done to save you, or you will be lost for ever.

And now do you ask WHAT IT IS TO REPENT? This is what I am going to tell you. If you leave off doing wrong because you feel that it is wicked to do wrong, that is repenting. If you feel that it is very wicked to get angry, to disobey your parents, and to tell lies, and stop doing these things, then you repent. If you feel that you have often offended God by having a bad temper, and by not minding what he says in the Bible, and if you are truly grieved that you have been so bad, and begin to hate your wrong doings, and to obey what God tells you, trusting in Christ for salvation, that is repentance. If you *cease to do evil, and learn to do well*, then you repent. If you feel that you are a guilty sinner, and that the only way of pardon is to come to Christ, and trust in him, and then with deep humility cast yourself on his mercy, having a sincere desire to love and serve him the remainder of your life—that will be to have true repentance.

Some people think that repentance is only being sorry that they have sinned. They say that if they are very sorry for their bad conduct, then they have repentance. But this is not always true. You may be very sorry that you have done wrong, because your parents have found it out, and you fear they will punish you, and not because you have been wicked in the sight of God. Such kind of sorrow is not repentance. You may be very sorry that you are a sinner, because you are afraid that God will punish you for your sins, and not because it is wrong to be a sinner. Your sorrows may come from thinking that God knows your sins. If he did not know, or if he would not punish, you might not be sorry at all that you had been wicked. Such sorrow is not repentance. I will tell you a story of a man who had this kind of sorrow, and it did him no good. It is a story from the Bible.

You have read in that holy book about the death of Jesus Christ. You remember what *Judas* did. He was one of the twelve disciples. But though he lived with Jesus, and pretended to love him, yet his heart was not right with God. He loved money too much, and was not honest in getting it. The Bible says he was a *thief.* He stole what belonged to other people. It is likely that he did thus wickedly for a long time before the other disciples knew his bad conduct. They thought he was a good man ; and he was not sorry, nor did he pretend to repent, till he was found out in his wickedness. But Judas grew worse and worse, as all men do who go in ways of sin and refuse to repent. When Jesus was eating his last supper with his twelve disciples, he said unto them, "One of you will betray me." They were sad at that saying, and began to ask which of them would do this wicked thing. One said, "Is it I ?" and another, "Is it I ?" They did not know which of them would do it. And as they all, except Judas, loved Jesus, they could not bear to think that any of them should do wrong to their good and kind Master. But the wicked man was sitting there with the good men. It was Judas. He had done wrong so many times, and had been a vile man so long, that he was ready to do any thing bad when he was displeased, and when he could get a little money by it. So he went to those unbelieving Jews who wanted to kill Jesus, and told them if they would give him some money, he would inform them where to find Jesus, that they might take him in the night. They said they would give him *thirty pieces of silver* if he would show them where Jesus was. So he took the money, and then led a band of soldiers to the place where Jesus had gone. It was night, and Jesus and his good disciples were in the garden of Gethsemane. They often went to that garden to pray. This night Jesus was troubled in his mind. He knew the time was come when he should be crucified for the sins of men. He prayed to God in a very earnest manner, saying, " O, my Father, if it be possible, let this cup pass from me ; nevertheless, not as I will, but as thou wilt." He was in such distress that "his sweat was as great drops of blood." When Judas had pointed out Jesus to the soldiers, they took hold of him and led him away to the palace of the high-priest.

From that place they sent him bound with cords to Pilate the Roman governor. Then the cruel soldiers mocked Jesus; they spit upon him; they struck him with their hands; they put a crown of thorns upon his head; they scourged him: that is, they whipped him with a whip made of many cords. Pilate thought that Jesus was a good man, but he at length gave orders that he should be killed—that he should be crucified, which was a very cruel kind of death. Then the soldiers nailed the hands and feet of Jesus to a cross, and raised him up in the air, and there he hung till he died.

O look at that sight! See Jesus on the cross, bleeding and dying. That death was a sacrifice for sin. That death made THE ATONEMENT. There you and I, and all sinners must look for pardon. No one can be saved without trusting in that redeeming work of Jesus Christ. No one can obtain pardon and eternal life, but by confiding in the merits of that Saviour who thus suffered and died on our behalf. You must look to him, if you would have mercy. " The blood of Jesus Christ cleanseth from all sin." You must feel that you need an interest in that redeeming blood. You must feel that you are a guilty sinner, and that there is no way of escape from the wrath of God but by coming to Christ, and trusting in the merits of his atoning sacrifice. And here, at the cross of Christ, is the place to repent. This is the place to have your heart broken, your will bound, and your soul renewed. Look then to the cross of Christ, that you may have true repentance ; not such repentance as Judas had, who was sorry for what he had done, but did not humble himself before God—but that "repentance which is unto life, and which needeth not to be repented of."

When Judas saw that they were going to crucify the Saviour, he began to be sorry for what he had done. Perhaps he did not think, when he first promised to betray his Master, that they would kill him ; and when he found that they would do it, he was sorry that he led the soldiers to take him. But though he was sorry, yet he did not truly repent. He had, as the Bible says, a certain kind of repentance. He was sorry that his bad conduct had brought evil on himself. He knew that what he had done was very wicked. He felt that every body would blame him, and call him a bad man.

He knew also, that he deserved to be punished, and was afraid of the wrath of God. For these things he was sorry. But this was not repenting. If he had truly repented, he would have run to Jesus while he was hanging on the cross, and would have begged to be forgiven. But instead of doing this, "he went and hanged himself." If he had truly repented, he would have become a good man, he would have prayed to God to pardon him, and then he would have commenced doing good, as the other disciples did, trying to save men from sin and from hell. But instead of this, he remained a wicked man, and went and took away his own life. This last act added greatly to his guilt, and showed that his sorrow, though it was very great, was not repentance.

Now every one of my young readers can see by this example, that there may be a great deal of sorrow and trouble of mind, without any repentance. God has said that he will punish you for your sins, if you do not repent. You may be exceedingly sorry that by sinning you have brought yourself into danger of a dreadful punishment, and yet you may still love to sin, and keep on sinning. Such sorrow is good for nothing. It has nothing like repentance in it. When you truly repent, you will *hate* sin, and will strive to do all that God commands you to do. If Judas had truly repented, he would not only have hated his bad conduct, and left it off, but he would have loved the Saviour and obeyed his commands. If he had repented with his whole heart, he would have been a good and pious man afterwards as long as he lived. He would not have taken his own life, and thus added the guilt of self-murder to all his other crimes.

By this time, my young reader, you begin to understand what it is to repent, if you have read carefully, and thought about what you have been reading. You see that repenting is *leaving off doing wrong because it is wrong, and doing right because it is right*—because God commands it, and it is pleasing to him. But I hope to make the subject still plainer before I have done writing; and I hope you will know still more about it before you have done reading this little book.

CHAPTER II.

FIRST STORY—FALSE REPENTANCE.

I WILL now relate two stories about two boys, who were very different from each other, as you will see.   James Cole was a smart, active lad, had a lively and cheerful mind, and was a leader among other boys in their amusements.   All the scholars in the school wanted James to be with them when they were out at their plays, he was so brisk in his sports, and ready in planning what they should do.   And yet it could hardly be said that they loved him, for he wanted every body to mind him, and was often fretful, and would sometimes get very angry.   But his worst fault was, that he would often deceive his playmates, and frequently tell lies.   The road where James went to school passed by a farmer's field, in which there was one season a large number of melons.   James had often looked through the fence to see these melons while they were growing, and thought he should take some of them when they got ripe.   Now this farmer was a very kind man, and would have given the boy a melon at any time when they had become ripe.   But James thought he would help himself to some of them, that is, he would *steal* them. He knew it was wrong to steal, but he thought that no one would find it out, and he did not think that God would see the wickedness, and punish him for it. He was a boy that did not think much about God, or heaven, or hell. When he did wrong, all that he cared for was that nobody in this world should know it.

At length the melons were ripe; and one evening after dark James climbed over the fence, and felt round on the ground till he found two large melons, which he took, one under each arm, and carried to his father's barn. There he ate what he wanted of them, and hid the rest for another time. In two or three days he had eaten them up, and began to think of getting some more. The farmer had found out that some one had been stealing his melons, for as James had felt around in the dark to find them, he trampled on the vines and broke them, and thus left the marks of what he had done. The farmer did not know who had stolen his melons, but thought perhaps the thief might come again; so he concluded to watch the field a little for several nights.

When James went the second time, and had just got hold of one melon, he heard some one coming, and seizing it quickly, he ran with all his might with the melon under his arm. Being a very active boy, he jumped over the fence and got away from the farmer, who was rather old and clumsy. But the farmer came near enough to him to know who he was. James ran all the way home, and fearing that the farmer would follow him, he did not stay to eat his melon, but hid it quickly in the barn, and then went with haste to bed.

Early the next morning the farmer went to James' father and told him that his son had been stealing melons. Mr. Cole was very much grieved to think that his son had been guilty of such wicked conduct, and he called James and asked him if he had done it. James said, No. He lied about it; for he thought the farmer would not be able to prove that he stole the melons. And he was so accustomed to tell lies that it did not trouble him at all to do it. When James said he did not get the fruit, his father told the farmer that he must have mistaken some other boy for James. But the farmer knew he was not mistaken, and he charged the blame on this boy so much that both James and his father were greatly offended. After much dispute, the farmer thought of a plan to make the matter sure, and to convince Mr. Cole that his son was guilty. He judged that James did not eat the melon the night before, and that by looking about he might be able to find it. So he went to searching, and after a while he found it, where James had put it, in the barn. And he not only found the melon which James had stolen the night before, but he found also the rinds of the melons which he had before stolen. "Here," said the farmer, calling Mr. Cole to come, "here is the melon, and the skins of the other ones; here is proof that I am right in saying that James is guilty of stealing." Mr. Cole was now convinced that his son had done it, and the farmer, without saying another word, went home.

After the farmer was gone, Mr. Cole and James talked together in the following manner.

MR. COLE. My son, I find you have been guilty of stealing and lying, and it grieves me to think you have been such a wicked boy. Are you sorry for it?

JAMES. Yes, father, I am sorry.

Mr. C. What are you sorry for?

James. I am sorry that the farmer came here and found out that I got his melons, and I am sorry that you feel bad about it.

Mr. C. And should you not be sorry, if the farmer had not come, and if the melons had not been found, and if I were not grieved?

James. I don't know as I should.

Mr. C. Ought you not to be sorry that you have done wrong, and have sinned against God?

James. I don't know but I ought.

Mr. C. My son, you ought to know that you have been very wicked, and that you have offended God. I must punish you for your bad conduct.

James. Why, the farmer had a great many melons, and I got only three.

Mr. C. But you ought not to have *stolen* any. If you had got but one, it would have been stealing; and stealing is wicked, whether you steal little or much. Besides, you have been guilty of lying, and told the lie a great many times over. What excuse can you have for that?

James. I hoped you would not find it out.

Mr. C. So, if I had not found it out, you would not have cared any thing about it?

JAMES. I don't know as I should.

MR. C. O, my son, how hard and stubborn you are in wickedness. I fear that God will punish you, for he says that " all liars shall have their part in the lake that burneth with fire and brimstone." You ought to humble yourself before God and repent.

JAMES. I do repent.

MR. C. What makes you think that you re· pent ?

JAMES. Because I am sorry.

MR. C. But would you have been sorry if your stealing and lying had not been found out?

JAMES. I don't know as I should.

MR. C. Then you do not feel right, my son. You are sorry, not because you have been a very wicked boy, but because you have been found out in your evil doings. This is not true repentance. God knew you had done wrong before the farmer and I knew it; and if you were truly penitent, you would be far more sorry that you offended God, than you are that we know it.

JAMES. Well, father, I am sorry that I have offended God.

Mr. C. Why are you sorry that you have offended God?

James. Because I am afraid he will punish me.

Mr. C. So, if you were not afraid that God would punish you, then you would not care any thing about it?

James. No, perhaps I should not.

Mr. C. Then you do not truly repent. You are not sorry for your wickedness; you are not grieved to think that you have a bad heart, and have been guilty of evil conduct; but you are troubled only because your evil doings have been found out, and you are afraid of punishment. This is not true repentance. I feel sad about you, my son; for unless you have better feelings than these, God will not forgive you, and you will grow worse and worse while you live, and when you die you will be wretched for ever.

After talking some time longer, Mr. Cole told James to go directly to the farmer, and ask his pardon. James hated to do this, and at first refused to go. His father told him that if he did not do it without delay, he should take a rod and punish him severely. James thought he would rather go to the farmer than receive such a punishment. So he went and

asked pardon. But it was plain that he did it
in a sour, unwilling manner. He was not
humble ; he had no proper feeling of his guilt.
This the farmer saw clearly enough ; but being
a kind man, he told the boy that he would forgive him. " But," said he, " if you are not
more humble and penitent before God, he will
not forgive you." James did not mind this,
for he only went to the farmer's to avoid the
whipping, and having escaped that, he did not
seem to care for any thing else.

When James went to school again, he was
more unpleasant in his temper than ever. He
was cross, did not restrain his angry passions,
and would often abuse his playmates. Now it
was plain from this, that he did not truly repent of his sins of stealing and lying. For if
he had truly repented of those sins, he would
have repented of all other sins. He would
have been more mild and humble in his temper than he used to be. He would have been
more kind and peaceful. He would have loved
his playmates better, and they would have
loved him better than ever. But there was
nothing of this. He was plainly worse, in all
respects, than he was before.

All my young readers see that James did not truly repent. And yet he was sorry, very sorry, that he stole the melons and told the lies. He wept much about it while his father was talking with him, and he wished a thousand times that he had not done so. But his tears were shed because he had been detected in his wickedness. His wishes that he had not done so, arose from fear of being punished. He did not humble himself before God, and pray that he might have "a new heart and a right spirit." He did not humble himself before his father, whom he had grieved, nor before the farmer, whom he had wronged. The same proud and stubborn spirit which he had before, he still had. It is certain, therefore, that he did not truly repent.

Some people, if they had seen James crying, and saying he was sorry, would have said that he repented. But we must have other proof besides sorrow and tears, to convince us that a sinner repents. His feelings and conduct must be changed. He must be, as the Bible says, "a new creature." His former sinful feelings and conduct he must hate, and he must do right, must begin to obey and serve God in earnest. Then he repents, and not before.

CHAPTER III.

SECOND STORY—TRUE REPENTANCE.

Now for the story about the other boy. His name was Samuel Gale. He had no father or mother; they both died when he was a little child, and he did not remember any thing about them. He lived with Mr. Smith, a very kind gentleman, who had taken the orphan boy, and treated him as a son. Samuel was a modest and sober lad, not much inclined to play, and not very active in his motions. He was not cheerful enough to be a pleasant playmate, and the other boys did not like him very well, for they said he was always sad, and always thinking about something. And it must be owned, that he was rather easy to get offended, and was sometimes peevish and fretful. But with all these faults, Samuel was a very good boy to learn. He loved his studies, and was very fond of reading his Sabbath-school books, and such other books as he could get.

Mr. Smith had a peach-tree in his garden, and one summer it was loaded with very fine fruit. Wishing to have the peaches get fully ripe, he gave strict orders to all his family not to pluck any of them from the tree, till he should tell them they might. Samuel, who was often in the garden, watched the peaches as they were getting ripe, and changing their color. When they began to put on their yellow coat, they looked very beautiful, and Samuel longed to get a taste of them. One day he found that one had fallen from the tree. It was a very large and fair one. Taking it up in his hand, he thought it would not be wrong to eat it, as he did not pick it from the tree. So he ate it, and it was so exceedingly good, that he had a strong desire to get some more of them. However, he restrained himself at that time from taking any. But he kept thinking all the afternoon how good the peach tasted, and how many other good ones there were on the tree. In the evening, when it began to grow dark, he went into the garden again, and thought to himself that he might get a few of the peaches, and nobody would know it. He knew it would be wrong, and sometimes he determined that he would not do it. But as he stayed about the tree, he felt his appetite grow keener, and at length he gave way to the temptation, and said he would have some of the fruit. As he could not reach the peaches while standing on the ground, he climbed up into the tree. The shaking of the tree made some of the fruit fall to the ground, and as it was now dark, and he could not see the peaches, but was obliged to feel about with his hand to find them, he knocked off a good many. And now he began to be sorry that he had climbed the tree. He had knocked off so many, that he feared Mr. Smith would find out that somebody had been there. But, poor boy, a worse thing still was about to happen to him. In his haste to get down, he stepped with his whole weight on a large limb, already loaded with fruit, and the limb broke, and he fell to the ground. The fall hurt him some, but he did not care for that. What troubled him then, was, that he had left so many marks of what he had done, that he feared he should be found out as the rogue. He was so sorry that he had meddled with the tree, that he could not eat a single peach; so he took out all that he had put into his pockets and threw them on the ground. He went into the house, and soon after went to bed.

This was a sad night for Samuel. He could

not sleep. He lay uneasy in his bed, and blamed himself for his folly. As he lay thinking what he should do, he sometimes almost concluded that he would get up in the morning, and go directly to Mr. Smith, tell him what he had done, confess his faults, and beg forgiveness. This would have been right, but he was not penitent enough to do it. At other times, he thought it might not be known that he did it, and so he might save himself the disgrace of confessing. There was a hard struggle in his mind. He wept much, and sleep departed from his eyes.

When the morning came, and Samuel arose from his restless bed, if he had gone at once to Mr. Smith, and confessed his faults, and become a good boy, and obeyed his master, and served God ever afterwards, that would have been repentance. But though he thought some of doing this, yet he was not humble enough to be willing to do it. He felt that he should be ashamed if he confessed his fault. So he did not then repent, though he was very sorry that he had done the wicked deed, and shed a great many tears about it.

Soon after breakfast, Mr. Smith went into

the garden, and saw one of the large limbs of his peach-tree broken off, and many of the peaches scattered about on the ground. The sight made him sad, and almost angry. He went into the house, and said that some one had been stealing the peaches, and had nearly spoiled the tree. Samuel dreaded to hear him speak, and thought if Mr. Smith should ask him if he did it, he would say he did not. Ah, this was a bad thought; he did not at that moment consider, that telling a lie about it would be as bad as getting the peaches, and even worse. Samuel was not apt to tell lies, but he had done it a few times, and now concluded to do it again. So, when Mr. Smith asked his family if any one had been getting the peaches, they all said they had not; and Samuel, too, said he had not. If Mr. Smith had observed closely when Samuel spoke, he would have seen a blush of shame, and the marks of guilt in his face. But as he had always been a pretty good boy, and had seldom been caught in a lie, Mr. Smith concluded that somebody else had done it. He asked his family who they thought it might be. They all guessed that it was Thomas Reed, a boy in

the neighborhood, who had often been guilty
of such deeds.

Samuel felt glad for a moment, that he had
not been found out. He soon left the room;
but when he was alone, his mind was much
troubled. His lie now gave him as much pain
as the other trespass. All the forenoon his
feelings were very painful. Sometimes he
tried to excuse himself, but he knew there was
no excuse, and his trying to do it made him
appear worse in his own sight. Once he
thought to excuse his lie in this way. He
said, " Mr. Smith asked if I *had been getting
the peaches.* I told him, no ; and I did not
get any of them, for I left them all under the
tree." But this plan quieted his mind only for
a moment; for he knew that he did get his
pockets full of the peaches, and only left them
under the tree because the limb broke. He
knew himself, he *felt* himself guilty. No ex-
cuses could satisfy his mind. He was uneasy
and wretched.

In the afternoon, while Mr. Smith and some
of his neighbors were looking at the broken
peach-tree, Thomas Reed and his father came
along They called Mr. Reed and his son into

the garden, and charged the boy with robbing the tree. Thomas denied it, as well he might. But one of the men said he saw Thomas looking through the fence at the tree the day before. This statement, and the fact that he had often been guilty of theft and other bad conduct, made them all think that Thomas was the rogue. So Thomas' father took a large rod, and gave him a severe whipping. Samuel saw the blows, and feeling that he deserved them himself, he was more unhappy than ever. He almost concluded, when he saw Thomas smarting under the rod, to run to them and confess that he was the guilty boy, and so save Thomas. But he was not yet humble enough to do it. So he ran away by himself alone, and cried much about his own guilt and Thomas' suffering. But still, this was not repenting, *for he did not do what he knew he ought to do.* This was proof that he did not yet repent ; for you must remember that every true penitent *will do what he knows he ought to do.*

Samuel did not sleep much more this night than he did the night before. He felt that he was more guilty now than he was the last night. He went to his bed with a sad heart.

As he lay there, uneasy and weeping, he
thought of a great many things that he had
done in his past life, which were wrong. He
seemed to remember all his wicked feelings
and conduct. Before this time, he used to
think himself a very good boy, and did not feel
that he was a great sinner. But now it seemed to him that his whole life had been wicked.
He felt that his heart was full of evil. While
he lay restless and unhappy on his bed, he
remembered what the Bible says: "The wicked are like the troubled sea that cannot rest,
whose waters cast up mire and dirt. There
is no peace, saith my God, to the wicked."
Samuel felt that all this is true. He thought
how often he had been disobedient, and fretful,
and angry. He remembered that he had been
guilty of lying before. He found that he had
been disobeying God all his days. These
thoughts troubled him much. "How foolish
and wicked I have been," he said. "I never
considered that I was such a sinner before."
Again he considered his late bad conduct. He
thought of the peach-tree, and his disobedience
and theft. He thought of the wicked lie he
had told. He thought, too, of Thomas Reed,

and seemed almost to hear him cry again, while suffering the stripes which he ought to have borne himself. His heart was full of anguish. He could endure it no longer. " I will confess," said he; " I will tell Mr. Smith. it was I that got the peaches, and broke the tree. I will tell him that I told a wicked lie about it. And I will go to Thomas Reed and beg his pardon."

Now Samuel was humble. Now he truly began his repentance. He was honest in what he said, and was resolved to do it as soon as the morning light should come. Now his mind was more at peace. Though his conduct seemed to him as bad as ever, yet he now resolved *to do what he knew he ought to do.* He did not think so much, at this time, whether Mr. Smith would forgive him, or whether God would forgive him ; but he resolved to confess and forsake his sins. This brought some quiet to his mind, and it being almost morning, he got a little sleep.

Early in the morning, he arose and kneeled down by his bedside, and confessed his sins, and prayed to God for some time. Samuel never prayed in such a manner before. There, on his knees before God, *he resolved to do all that he knew he ought to do,* and he prayed God to help him to keep this resolution as long as he lived. This was repenting. He went down to Mr. Smith's room, and as soon as Mr. Smith came in, he went and kneeled down at his feet, and said, "It was I that got the peaches. It was I that broke the tree. I told a very wicked lie about it. Thomas Reed was not to blame." Mr. Smith was very much surprised; and as Samuel seemed very humble and penitent, he said, "I will forgive you, my boy." As Samuel felt that he was almost too wicked to be forgiven, he hardly thought Mr. Smith would pardon him so soon. He felt that he deserved punishment, and was willing to be punished. But he was glad to hear the words of pardon, and he thought he should love Mr. Smith better than he ever did, and should not disobey him again. All the family were glad to see Samuel so penitent, and they all most fully forgave him.

He then asked Mr. Smith if he might go before breakfast and see Thomas Reed. Mr Smith gave him leave, and he ran with great haste over to Mr. Reed's. As soon as he found

Thomas, he said to him, " I knew you did not
get the peaches.   I was sorry to see you punished yesterday.   I was the one to blame."
Thomas was rather cross, but Samuel asked
his pardon a good many times, and told him
that he would always do him all the good in
his power.   He then went home, praying to
God as he walked along, that, for Christ's
sake, he would forgive him, and make him
ever after a good and pious boy.

We have reason to believe that God heard
the prayers of Samuel, and granted his re-
quest; for he was very much changed, and
was in all respects a much better boy afterwards.   He remembered his promise, to *do
every thing which he knew he ought to do.*
He read his Bible much more than he used to
do, and the more he read that holy book, the
better he loved it.   He spent a short season
two or three times a day, in earnest prayer to
God.   His temper was better than it was before.   He was more cheerful and happy, and
his schoolmates, and all who knew him, loved
him better.   After a few months, he thought
that he ought to obey the Lord Jesus Christ,
in making a public profession of religion, and

confess him before men. So he was united with the church, and he lived ever afterwards such a blameless and pious life, that every body believed he was a Christian.

Here, my young readers, you see what true repentance is. You see that it is *a confessing and forsaking of sin.* You see that when one repents, he is humble, he is not ashamed to confess his guilt. And you see, also, that when a person is in a state of mind to repent of *one* sin, he will repent of *all* sin. This last thing, I wish you always to remember. Many people deceive themselves on this point. They think they have repented of some very wicked act, because they are sorry for it, and intend not to do it again; while all their other feelings and conduct are not changed at all. It is plain, in such cases, that they do not truly repent of the *one* sin; for if they did, they would have a state of mind which would lead them to repent of *all* sin. This was the fact with Samuel. He first repented of his sin of robbing the peach-tree, and lying about it. But as soon as his mind was in a humble and penitent state, he repented of all sin, and was much changed in all his feelings and habits. His repentant state of mind showed that he was what the Scriptures call "a new creature."

Another thing, which I want all my young readers to remember, is, that when any one repents, *he will be ready to do his duty.* This is so important a thought, that I have before mentioned it several times in other words, and I may repeat it again before the close of the book. Some people seem to think that they have repented of a sin, or of all their sins, while they neglect many duties. They do not observe all the duties of religion. They seldom read the Bible; they neglect prayer; they refuse to obey the commands of the Saviour; they do not live pious and Christian lives. Yet they think they have often repented of sin. But it is not so. They deceive themselves. If they had repented of one sin, they would repent of all sin. If they had repented of any sin, they would obey God in the duties of religion. If they had penitent hearts, *they would endeavor to do all that they know they ought to do.*

CHAPTER IV.

BIBLE EXAMPLES—PETER.

Now, as I have finished the stories about the two boys, I will again take the Bible, and give you an account of the repentance of Peter, and David, and the Prodigal Son. Bible stories are, after all, the best stories, for they are such as God has given us, and it is said in the Psalms, that the word of God is " a lamp unto our feet, and a light unto our path." It teaches us truly what we should believe, how we should feel, and what we should do. It will instruct us plainly what true repentance is, and how the good men it speaks of felt and acted when they repented.

I will begin with the story of PETER. You know that he was one of the twelve apostles of Jesus Christ. He was sometimes called Cephas, sometimes Simon, sometimes Simon Peter, but oftener Peter. He was the son of Jonas, and Andrew was his brother. The city where Peter lived was called Bethsaida. It was situated on the coast of the sea of Galilee, or, as it is sometimes called, the sea of Tiberias, or the lake of Gennesaret. Peter was a fisherman. As the Lord Jesus was walking one day by the side of this sea, he saw two brothers, Peter and Andrew, casting a net into the sea, to catch some fishes. Jesus said to them, "Follow me, and I will make you fishers of men." He meant, that he would make them ministers, to preach unto men, and gather them into his kingdom. The two brothers immediately left their nets and followed Jesus. All men, and even young persons, when they are invited to come to Christ, should do as these brothers did. They should immediately become the followers of Christ; that is, they should be *Christians*. And this is what I want all my young readers to be.

Peter was a man of very warm feelings and quick passions. He was an ardent man, that is, warm, active, and zealous; and before he was fully under the influence of the meek and humble spirit of religion, he was apt to be hasty in his temper and actions, and he often did wrong. I am going to tell you about one very wrong and wicked thing which he did, and how he repented of it, and became a very good and holy man. But I must first speak of some things which show how kind the Saviour was to him, and which made it more wicked for Peter to deny him as he did.

Jesus was very kind to Peter in calling him to be his follower, when he might have passed by him, and called some other man. It was a great privilege to be a disciple, and it was more wicked for one who had this privilege, to be guilty of a bad act, than for one who was not a disciple. And here, I want my young readers to remember one thing. It is this: it is more wicked for *you* to do wrong, than it is for the heathen, who do not know about the Saviour, and who have not the Bible. You have often read about the Saviour; you are called to be his followers; you have a Sabbath-school, and kind teachers, and a good minister, to teach and call you to repentance; you have great privileges, and if you do wrong, if you refuse to repent, you are far more wicked than heathen children and youths. It was because Peter was called into the family of Jesus, and had such good teachings and examples, that his crime in denying him was so very great.

Jesus was also very kind in choosing him, and James, and John, to be with him at certain times and places, where the other disciples were not permitted to be. At these seasons, they saw and heard many important things, which the other disciples did not see and hear. Peter was one of the three who went with Jesus to the mountain, when he " was transfigured before them, and his face did shine as the sun, and his raiment was white as the light. And behold, there appeared unto them Moses and Elias, talking with Jesus. Then said Peter unto Jesus, Lord, it is good for us to be here. Let us make here three tabernacles; one for thee, one for Moses, and one for Elias. And while he yet spake, behold, a bright cloud overshadowed them, and behold, a voice out of the cloud, which said, This is my beloved Son, in whom I am well pleased ; hear ye him." Now it was a great privilege for Peter to be there. He said himself, "Lord, it is *good* for us to be here." For this, he ought to have loved the Saviour more ; and it made it more wicked for him to deny him. Surely, when Peter was treated with so much honor and kindness, he ought to have loved his Master more than any of his fellow-disciples did ; and for him to say afterwards *that he did not know him*, was a very great sin.

I will now speak of those things which took place on the night when Peter denied his Master. It was a very solemn time, and many things were done that night which will be remembered for ever. In the early part of the evening, Jesus and his disciples ate the last supper together. While they were at the table, Jesus told them that one of them would betray him. They were all astonished and grieved at this; and Peter made a motion to John, who was lying on Jesus' bosom, that he should ask him who it was that should do this thing. John asked Jesus who it was, and Jesus pointed out Judas as the traitor. "As they were eating, Jesus took bread and blessed it, and brake it, and gave it to the disciples, and said, Take, eat; this is my body. And he took the cup and gave thanks, and gave it to them, saying, Drink ye all of it; for this is my blood of the new testament, which is shed for many, for the remission of sins. This do in remembrance of me." Thus was the sacrament of the Lord's supper appointed, and all pious people were told to partake of it in remembrance of the Saviour. When the supper was ended, Judas left the company of Jesus and his disciples, never more to join them. He went to the high-priest's palace, and agreed to betray Jesus to his enemies.

After Judas had gone, Jesus talked a long time with his disciples. As this was the last conversation with them before his death, his words seemed very precious to them. And truly, *never man spake like this man.* You can read what he said in the 14th, 15th, and 16th chapters of John. He then prayed with them, and his prayer is given in the 17th chapter of John. But though Jesus spoke and prayed in a most useful and affecting manner, yet he was very sorrowful. One of his disciples had gone to betray him, and the others, ne knew, would leave him when his enemies had laid hold of him. He told them, "All ye shall be offended because of me this night." But Peter said, "Though all men should be offended because of thee, yet will I never be offended." Peter then thought that he should never do any thing against his Master. But Jesus told him plainly that he would deny him. "Verily, I say unto thee, that this night, before the cock crow, thou shalt deny me thrice." Still, Peter thought he should not do it, and he said, "Though I should die with thee, yet will I not deny thee." But alas, Peter felt too confident. He trusted too much in his own strength. He did not, at that time, feel how weak he was, and that if he did not watch and pray, and get help from God, he would do very wickedly.

Then they all went over the brook Cedron, and came unto the garden of Gethsemane. Here Jesus had often been with his disciples. They seem to have chosen this place to get away from the noise and tumult of the city, so that they might talk and pray together, without having a multitude around them. When they had come into the garden, most of the disciples stopped in one place, and Jesus took Peter, and James, and John, and went a short distance to another place. You see, Peter was again chosen, and treated with much regard and kindness, though he was about to deny his Master. Jesus told the three disciples "to tarry there, and watch and pray," while he withdrew from them a little, to pray by himself alone. And now the Saviour was in great anguish of mind. He said, "My soul is exceeding sorrowful, even unto death." Being

in an agony, he prayed, and said, "O, my
Father, if it be possible, let this cup pass from
me; nevertheless, not my will, but thine be
done." After he had prayed, he came to the
disciples, and found them asleep; and he said
unto Peter, "What, could ye not watch with
me one hour?" Jesus went three times, and
prayed in the same manner, and each time,
when he returned, he found them sleeping
He was grieved that they did not watch an*
pray with him, and he gently rebuked them.

But while he was speaking to them, " Behold, Judas came, and with him a great multitude, with swords and staves, from the chief
priests and elders of the people." All this
multitude came out to take Jesus. Judas, the
wicked traitor, knew where to find him, and
as soon as he let them know which Jesus was,
they came near to lay their hands upon him.
Then Peter drew a sword to defend his Master,
and he smote a servant of the high-priest, and
cut off his ear. *Now*, Peter was full of zeal
to keep his Master from being taken. He
would, no doubt, at that moment, have given
up his own life, rather than have them carry
off the Saviour. Little did Peter then think,

that he should, in a very short time, say that
he never knew him. Jesus said to Peter,
"Put up thy sword." Then he gave himself
up to those who had come to take him. When
they had Jesus in their power, they led him
away to the palace of the high-priest; *and
Peter followed, afar off.*

Now was the hour of Peter's danger. The
time of trial had come. As he passed along
towards the palace, and saw the wicked rabble
leading his Master with rough and cruel hands,
he had many sad and strange thoughts. Perhaps, at this time, he began to doubt whether
Jesus was the true Saviour. He was disappointed. He did not think that Jesus would
let his enemies take him in this manner. Once,
when the people of Nazareth, in a great rage,
led forth Jesus to the brow of a hill to cast
him down headlong, he escaped from them in
a wonderful manner, and "passed through the
midst of them." Perhaps Peter thought he
would do so now. But Jesus made no attempt
to get away. "He was led as a lamb to the
slaughter, and as a sheep before her shearers
is dumb, so he opened not his mouth." Peter
was surprised at this. He thought that Jesus

might have put forth his mighty power and overcome his enemies; and because he did not do it, because he did not try to get away from them, it may be that Peter was offended with him. This was a wrong state of mind, and it led him to do a wicked act.

When they had all come into the high-priest's palace, Peter saw that his Master was now in the power of his enemies, and he gave up all for lost. And now he, who had a little while before drawn his sword to defend his Master, was ashamed to own him. As he was standing by the fire warming himself, a certain damsel saw him, and said, " Thou wast with Jesus of Galilee. But Peter denied before them all, saying, I know not what thou sayest. And when he was gone out into the porch, another maid saw him, and said unto them that were there, This fellow was also with Jesus of Nazareth. And again Peter denied with an oath, I do not know the man. And after a while came unto him they that stood by, and said to Peter, Surely thou art one of them. Then began he to curse and to swear, saying, *I know not the man.*" Oh, Peter, Peter, how art thou fallen! Is this the man to whom the Saviour had been so kind, and on whom he had bestowed so many favors? Is this the man who said, " Though I should die with thee, yet will I not deny thee?" Alas, what a change; how was Peter fallen!

After he had, in this wicked and profane manner denied his Master, Jesus turned and looked on Peter. That *look*—how it must have pierced him to his very soul. " And immediately the cock crew. And Peter remembered the words of Jesus which he said unto him, Before the cock crow, thou shalt deny me thrice. *And he went out and wept bitterly.*" Now Peter began to repent. He not only wept, but he wept *bitterly.* His repentance did not consist merely of weeping; he *changed his conduct.* He had denied his Master, but he did so no more. In a few days afterwards he *confessed* him before thousands on the day of Pentecost. He had been guilty of lying; afterwards he told the *truth*, though he exposed his own life by doing it. He had been guilty of swearing; but afterwards he used his tongue in praising the Saviour, and urging all men to love and serve him. If Peter had done nothing but shed tears, it would not have been repenting. His crying might have shown that he was sorry, but it would not have shown that he would be a good man. If he had wept till he had died, it would not have been repentance, so long as he refused to own the Saviour, and confess him before men. He had done wrong; *now he did right;* this was repenting.

From the time when Peter was guilty of the great sin of denying his Master, he spent his whole life in confessing him, and in urging his fellow-men to believe in Jesus and obey his commands. Thus it may be said, he repented all his days. The kind Saviour forgave him, and he was very useful in calling other men to repentance, and in building up the kingdom of Christ.

My young reader, has this story about Peter been interesting to you? I hope it has. And I hope also it will be profitable to you. I want you should become better by reading it. Do you think that you have ever denied the Saviour? I am afraid you have, many times. You have not denied him just as Peter did. You have not seen him. You have not told the Jews that you knew not the man. But you have been ashamed to confess Jesus before men; you have not prayed to him, and loved

him, and obeyed him as you ought to have
done. If you are not pious, you do still refuse
to own Jesus as *your* Saviour, and you do still
refuse to be his follower and friend. What is
this but denying him? Oh, my young reader,
you have been guilty, and you too ought to
repent. Like Peter, you must weep over your
sins, and not only weep, but change your conduct, and *do every thing that you know you
ought to do.* That would be repentance, and
then the Saviour would pardon you, and you
would be useful in the world and happy in
heaven.

Remember, that the way to be saved is to
repent of sin and trust in Christ. You must
see clearly that you are a sinner, guilty, de-
praved, and undone. You must feel that you
have disobeyed God, and denied the Saviour.
And a deep sense of guilt should humble you
to the dust. And when you are thus humbled,
when you see and feel that you are lost, and
when such a sense of your guilt and danger
leads you, through the influences of the Holy
Spirit, to reject all self-confidence, to abhor
yourself, and to trust alone in Christ for salvation, then you have true repentance.

CHAPTER V.

DAVID'S REPENTANCE.

THE next story which I promised to tell you
is about DAVID. This story, also, will be useful to my young readers, as I hope, showing
them what true repentance is. David was the
king of Israel. He was the son of Jesse, and
when he was young he kept his father's sheep.
He did not then think that he should ever be
a mighty man, and king over all Israel. I
cannot now stop to tell the manner in which
he rose from his low state to be the ruler of a
great nation. You can read all about it in the
Bible, in the first book of Samuel. I can only
say now, that when he was young his conduct
was very good. The Lord loved him and
blessed him, and when he became a man the
Lord made him king instead of Saul, who was
a wicked man.

After David had been king a long time, and
had done a great many good things, he was
tempted at one time to do a very wicked thing.
As he was walking one day on the roof of his
house, he saw a very beautiful woman, and he
wanted to have her. But she was the wife of

another man, and David had no right to take her to himself. She was the wife of Uriah the Hittite, and he was one of David's soldiers, and was then gone with the army to fight against the enemies of David. The woman's name was Bathsheba, and though she was married to another man, David resolved to have her himself. As he was king, and could do what he pleased, he sent and took her, and brought her into his own house. This was exceedingly wrong. It was wronging Bathsheba. It was ill-treating Uriah, her husband, who was a faithful soldier and friend of David. And it was sinning against God. But David, being a king, seemed to think that he had a right to do as he pleased, and for a long time he appears not to have had any proper sense of his guilt.

But he did not stop sinning when he had done this. One sin, as is commonly the case, prepared the way for another. He had got Bathsheba, and now he wanted to get rid of her husband. So he sent word to Joab, the commander of his army, to put Uriah "in the forefront of the hottest battle," and then to leave him, that he might be killed by the enemy. Joab did as the king bade him do,

and thus Uriah, the brave soldier, was killed.
Though David did not kill him with his own
hand, yet, as he planned his death and intended
to have him killed, he was guilty of murder.
He was now in a very sad and awful state; yet
he did not, for some time, seem to feel his guilt.
He was loaded with two black and frightful
crimes, yet for several months he did not appear to be sensible of his great sins. Alas,
how was he fallen!

At length, to bring him to a feeling of his
guilt, God sent a prophet to convince him of
his sin. The narrative is so good and interesting, that I will relate it as it is written in the
Bible. You may find it in 2d Samuel, chapter
12 : " The thing that David had done displeased
the Lord. And the Lord sent Nathan unto
David; and he came unto him, and said unto
him, There were two men in one city; the one
rich, and the other poor. The rich man had
exceeding many flocks and herds; but the poor
man had nothing save one little ewe-lamb,
which he had bought and nourished up : and
it grew up together with him, and with his
children ; it did eat of his own meat, and drank
of his own cup, and lay in his bosom, and was

unto him as a daughter. And there came a traveller unto the rich man, and he spared to take of his own flock and of his own herd, to dress for the way-faring man that was come unto him; but he took the poor man's lamb, and dressed it for the man that was come unto him. And David's anger was greatly kindled against the man; and he said unto Nathan, As the Lord liveth, *the man that hath done this thing shall surely die;* and he shall restore the lamb four-fold, because he did this thing, and because he had no pity. Then Nathan said to David, *Thou art the man.* Thus saith the Lord God of Israel, I anointed thee king over Israel, and I delivered thee out of the hand of Saul; and I gave thee thy master's house, and thy master's wives into thy bosom, and gave thee the house of Israel and of Judah; and if that had been too little, I would moreover have given thee such and such things. Wherefore hast thou despised the commandment of the Lord, to do evil in his sight? Thou hast killed Uriah the Hittite with the sword, and hast taken his wife to be thy wife, and hast slain him with the sword of the children of Ammon. Now therefore the sword shall never depart from thy house, because thou hast despised me, and hast taken the wife of Uriah the Hittite to be thy wife. Then David said unto Nathan, *I have sinned against the Lord.*"

Now David was made to feel himself guilty. Now he felt that he had done wickedly in the sight of God and man, and that his being a king was no excuse for his crime, but rather made it worse. His own mind condemned him. His conscience stung him with remorse. He was full of bitterness of spirit and anguish of soul. He fasted and wept and prayed before the Lord. *He repented.* But how did he repent? Were his tears his only repentance? No; he *changed his feelings and conduct.* Was his fasting and his lying all night on the ground, all his repentance? No; he sought a new state of mind, that he might be a good and holy man. He prayed to God in these words: " Create in me a clean heart, O God, and renew a right spirit within me." But did his prayers make all his repentance? No; he began to do the will of God. He left off doing wrong, and went to doing right. He tried to save others from sin. In his earnest and humble prayer to God, he says, " Then will I teach transgressors thy ways, and sinners shall be converted unto thee." You may see much how he felt and what he did, in the 51st Psalm, which he wrote at this time. Not only was he exceedingly sorry for his sin, but *he did so no more.* This changing his conduct was repentance. And he not only refused to commit such a great sin again, but he went on doing all that he knew he ought to do. This was repenting.

David lived a great many years afterwards, and was a very pious man and a good king. He wrote most of the book of Psalms. These contain the feelings of his heart, and it is easy to see, in reading them, that he had a penitent mind. But the evidence that he truly repented of his great sin, is found chiefly in his efforts to *be* good, and to *do* good the rest of his life. As he engaged in the service of God with all his heart, he was very useful in the work of religion. Being a king, his example had great influence over the nation, in leading others to do right. There were a great many pious men in Israel at that time; the worship of God was strictly regarded, and the duties of religion generally attended to. The people were moved

by the example and writings of the king, and
never was the nation of Israel so pious and
happy as in the days of David.

Thus have I given my young reader an account of the sin and of the repentance of David.
I have not tried to cover over his sin, and make it
appear less than it was. David himself did not
attempt to conceal it. He confessed it openly
before God and man. It was a great sin. But
his repentance was great too. He repented all
his days. He lived repenting, by doing good,
serving God, urging all men to repentance, and
being the means of saving many souls. This
is the kind of repentance which I want all my
young readers to have. You have not com-
mitted such a sin as David did, but you are a
sinner; you have done wrong a thousand times,
and you have neglected to do what you knew
was right. You have refused to love, and
obey, and follow the Saviour. For these sins
you must repent, or you will perish for ever.
And your repentance must be leaving off doing
wrong, and engaging in doing right. It is not
enough for you to say that you are sorry for
your sins. It is not enough for you to weep
because your sins expose you to the awful pun-

ishment which the Bible says that God will put upon the impenitent sinner. You must change your course of life. You must engage in the service of God. You must become a follower of Christ. This is the kind of repentance which you need. No other will do you any good.

Perhaps some one of my young readers will think in this manner: "Well, David was a great sinner, and he ought to repent; if I were as great a sinner as he was, I would repent too; but I never did any thing very bad." Stop, now, and let us see if you judge right in this matter. You say that you never did any thing very bad. Is it not very bad to tell lies, and have you not often done this? The Bible says, that "all liars shall have their part in the lake that burneth with fire and brimstone." Surely, God thinks that lying is a very great sin, when he has threatened so great a punishment against it. Say not, then, that you never did any thing bad. Is it not very bad to get angry? The Saviour said, "He that is angry with his brother without a cause, is in danger of the judgment." How many times you have been angry with others, without any just cause. Anger is the very spirit of a mur-

derer. Is it not, then, very wicked? The Bible
says, "He that hateth his brother is a murderer." It does not mean, that every one who
hateth another actually kills him. But it
means, that when you hate another, you have
the spirit of a murderer; you have a feeling
like that which leads one man to kill another.
And have you not many times felt anger and
hatred towards others? It is not right, then,
for you to say that you never did any thing very
bad. Besides, is it not very wicked to disobey
God, and not to mind what the Saviour says to
you? Yet you have refused to do what God
tells you to do in the Bible. The Saviour has
called you to come unto him; and yet, I fear
you have not done it. You have not minded
what he says when he invites you to become
his follower. Now think of it; are you not a
great sinner, when you have so long refused to
regard what Jesus says, and when you refuse
to obey God? Never think again that you
are not a great sinner; but go immediately in
humble prayer to God, and confess that your
sins are great, and beg of him to give you a new
heart, and a right spirit, and begin now to live a
Christian and pious life. This will be repenting.

CHAPTER VI.

THE PRODIGAL SON.

THE story of the PRODIGAL SON, which I will now relate to my young readers, is a most interesting and instructive parable, spoken by our Lord Jesus Christ. The main object of the Saviour, in giving this parable, was to show how willing and ready our heavenly Father is to forgive the repenting sinner. But the parable is very useful also in showing what repentance is, and how a sinner will feel and do when he repents. I must first relate the story in the language of Jesus himself, for no other words are so good as his words. You will find the parable in Luke, chapter 15.

"And he said, A certain man had two sons; and the younger of them said unto his father, Father, give me the portion of goods that falleth to me. And he divided unto them his living. And not many days after, the younger son gathered all together, and took his journey into a far country, and there wasted his substance with riotous living. And when he had spent all, there arose a mighty famine in that land, and he began to be in want. And he went and joined himself to a citizen of that country, and he sent him into his fields to feed swine. And he would fain have filled his belly with the husks that the swine did eat; and no man gave unto him. And when he came to himself, he said, How many hired servants of my father's have bread enough and to spare, and I perish with hunger! I will arise and go to my father, and will say unto him, Father, I have sinned against heaven, and before thee, and am no more worthy to be called thy son; make me as one of thy hired servants: and he arose, and came to his father. But when he was yet a great way off, his father saw him, and had compassion on him, and ran and fell on his neck, and kissed him. And the son said unto him, Father, I have sinned against heaven, and in thy sight, and am no more worthy to be called thy son. But the father said to his servants, Bring forth the best robe, and put it on him; and put a ring on his hand, and shoes on his feet. And bring hither the fatted calf, and kill it; and let us eat, and be merry: for this my son was dead, and is alive again; he was lost, and is found."

And is God thus willing to receive every

sinner who repents and returns to him? Yes.
The Saviour related the parable on purpose to
show that God is willing, and more than willing, to pardon the sinner who truly repents
and returns to his duty. O how full of kindness and mercy is our heavenly Father!

Let us now, in our thoughts, follow this
younger son as he left the home of his childhood, and wandered among strangers. Perhaps before he left home he thought the rules
of his father's house too strict. He imagined
that he did not have liberty enough. He
wanted to do as he pleased. So all sinners
feel when they wander away from God. They
think his laws too strict. They consider religion as a gloomy thing, and that it would
restrain them so much as to injure their happiness. They want to do as they please, and
not be obliged to obey the commands of God.
And so you feel, my young reader, when you
are unwilling to obey your parents, when you
think they might let you do as you please, and
when you refuse to obey God. Then you are
like the Prodigal, who wanted to get away
from his father's house. These are wicked
feelings, and they lead to wicked doings.

When the Prodigal had departed from his home, and had begun his course of guilty wandering, we may suppose him at first to be very merry. He says to himself, "Now I am at liberty; now I can do as I please. I shall no longer be obliged to mind the rigid rules of my father's house. I will seek out some merry companions, and we will enjoy ourselves without restraint and without fear. We shall be happy—we will indulge our appetites and passions, and take our fill of pleasure." Such were his dreams of happiness. These were the hopes which led him away from duty, and plunged him into wretchedness. He had not yet learned that restraint is needful for all human beings, and that obedience to holy laws is the only way to true happiness.

All sinners who seek their pleasures wholly in the things of this world, feel and act just as he did. They promise themselves much delight in their worldly pleasures. They are glad to be away from the paths of religion. They think they shall be happier without piety than with it. And if they could only think that God would not regard them, nor call them to an account for their conduct, it would fill them with joy. But such joys cannot last long; they lead quickly to pain and misery. My young reader, have you ever thought that you should be more happy if you could always do as you pleased, and if you were not obliged to mind your parents and obey God? I fear that you have sometimes thought so. If you have, you were like the Prodigal. Your sinful feelings have blinded and deceived you. You have wanted to go in a way that leads to guilt and wretchedness.

Just look again, now, and see how it happened to the Prodigal. Did he find the happiness he expected? Did he enjoy all those pleasures which he had promised himself? No; he was disappointed. It is true, he felt a short-lived joy when he began his sinful course. When he found his gay companions, the vile men and women with whom he " spent his substance in riotous living," for a moment he thought himself happy. He gave himself up to mirth and wicked pleasures. But this season of guilty joys was short. All his money was soon spent, " and he began to be in want." His gay companions left him in the time of his need. He found no friends to comfort him in his misfor-

tunes, or to supply him with food. In his distress he was obliged to submit to the degrading
business of feeding swine; and in his hunger
" he would fain have filled his belly with the
husks that the swine did eat." And what added greatly to his distress in this destitute and
degraded state, was, that " no man gave unto
him ;" no friendly hand was stretched out for
his relief—no one pitied him in his fallen and
starving condition.

Now I wish my young reader to observe how
plainly this wretched state of the prodigal shows
the condition of sinners, who have gone away
from God, and have been seeking happiness in
the things of this world. They can find nothing
on earth to satisfy the desires of their immortal souls. Though they may obtain much
worldly substance, and enjoy much earthly
pleasure, yet their souls are unfed. They have
no heavenly and spiritual food. They must
soon die and leave all they have got in this
world, and they are not prepared for heaven.
Such a state is wretched. Yet many sinners,
while in health and prosperity, do not feel their
wretchedness. I am afraid that some who read
this little book have never felt it. You have

wandered from your heavenly Father's house.
You have sinned against God.   You have none
of the hopes and joys of the true sons of God.
And you have no right to expect that you shall
go to heaven when you die.   And yet I fear
that you do not feel how miserable and guilty
your condition is.   O, that you might be brought
to a proper sense of it.   Then you would see
that you must repent, or perish for ever.

The poor prodigal *did* feel his wretched condition.   " When he came to himself "—there is
much meaning in this.   His love of worldly
pleasures had, as it were, made him crazy.   He
had been blinded and deluded.   He knew not
whither he was going.   False hopes deceived
him.   He sought happiness where it could not
be found.   But " when he came to himself, he
said, How many hired servants of my father's
have bread enough and to spare, and I perish
with hunger !"   It was then that he began to
think seriously about the *cause* of his wretchedness.   He found out the reason why he was
in this sad condition.   He saw his own folly
and guilt in leaving his father's house.   He
was fully convinced that he had chosen the
wrong way to gain happiness.   It was plain to

him that those laws and restraints which he once thought severe, were needful to make him do right, and that the only way to be happy is to *do right.* His mind began to be humbled. That pride which had led him to reject the counsels of his father and to choose his own way, he began to give up. He blamed himself. He lamented his folly and wept over his disgrace. He felt too, that he deserved all the evils that had come upon him, and much more. At this time, no doubt, he began to be a true penitent. We judge this, not simply because he was sensible of his guilt, and blamed himself, and wept over his sad condition, but because he now resolved to return to his duty. *He determined to do what he knew he ought to do.* This was proof that he had begun to repent in earnest. He was truly sorry that he had done wrong, and began at once to do right This was repentance. " I will arise," said he, " and go to my father, and will say unto him, Father, I have sinned against heaven, and before thee, and am no more worthy to be called thy son; make me as one of thy hired servants." And he then did as he said he would do. He came to his father. He did not know whether his father would receive him. But he would do his own duty. He did not claim to be received as a son, for he felt himself to be unworthy. The place of a hired servant was all that he asked, and better, he felt, than he deserved. This was true humility. Here was repentance.

Now, my young reader, if you will look steadily and thoughtfully at this example, you cannot fail to learn the nature of true repentance. You will see clearly how you must feel and act, that you may repent. You must feel that you have wandered away from your duty and your God. And have you not thus wandered? You must feel that you have been seeking happiness in the wrong way, that you have loved this world too much, and have gone after earthly trifles, and have neglected God and heaven. And is it not true that you have done so? You must feel that such a course of conduct is very wicked in the sight of God, that it is rebellion against him, and that you have been acting as his enemy. And is not all this true? If a child will not obey his father, but runs away from home and joins himself with other disobedient and wicked chil-

dren, and keeps on doing what his father told
him not to do, is not that child a rebel against
his father? And have you not thus refused to
obey God? Have you not departed from the
way in which he told you to go? Have you not
joined yourself with other sinners, who trans-
gress God's law? And does not such conduct
make you a rebel and an enemy against God?

You must feel, too, that you have brought
yourself into difficulty, that your condition is
a sad one, that you have forsaken the right way
to happiness, and have gone after foolish objects
and lying vanities. And can you not see that
you have done this? Is it not plain, that de-
parting from God and duty is the way to be
wretched and lost? But more than all, you
must feel yourself *guilty.* You have no excuse for disobeying God. It is wrong. It is
wicked. This you must feel, or you will never
repent. The prodigal felt it. He did not pretend to bring any excuse for his vile conduct.
He blamed *himself.* Such feelings you must
have. The blame of all your guilt and wretchedness, you must charge to your own account.
Like the prodigal you must, in sincere confes-
sion before God, say, " Father, I have sinned

against heaven, and in thy sight, and am no more worthy to be called thy son."

But, my young reader, you must not stop at this point. If you should lament your sad condition, and bewail your sins, and condemn yourself ever so much, it would do you no good, except you changed your course of life. Your sorrow for sin is not of the right kind unless it leads you to hate sin, and love holiness. Your sorrow that you have wandered away from God and brought yourself into a wretched and lost condition, will not be true repentance, unless you return to God and do your duty. Your grief when you think of your rebellion and guilt, will do you no good, unless you leave off your rebellion, and go in the way of God's commandments. You must " arise and go to your Father." You must return to him from whom you have gone away. His laws you must obey. His commandments you must do. In short, you must begin at once and in earnest to live a pious and Christian life. That will be true repentance.

Perhaps, my young reader, if you should begin to think seriously about your sinfulness, and should be deeply convinced of your guilt, and your mind should be much troubled about

it, you might be ready to think that there is no
help for you, and that you must perish. Many
sinners have had such feelings. They saw that
they *deserved* to perish, and concluded that
they should be lost, and that there was no
mercy for them. The parable of the Prodigal
Son shows that such feelings are not right.
We may learn in this parable, that God *will*
pardon all who truly repent and return to their
duty. He is more ready to forgive, than sinners are to repent. He will never refuse to
accept any who come unto him. When God
sent his own Son into the world to redeem man,
and when Jesus came and laid down his life as
a sacrifice for the sins of mankind, proof enough
was given that sinners might be saved. And
now that his atonement has been made, now
that the way has been opened for the pardon of
sinners, every one who feels his guilt and danger, and who repents and comes to Christ, will
be forgiven. God has promised this. Never
was a truly penitent soul rejected. " Him that
cometh unto me," said the Saviour, " I will in
no wise cast out." Here is ample encourage-
ment. You need not perish. If you feel that
your sins have ruined you, and that you have

no help in yourself, then go to Christ for help, and he will save you. Go to the Saviour who says, " The Son of man is come to seek and to save that which is lost," and you shall be forgiven and saved. You may rely on this. It is certain; for it is the promise of God.

But if it was uncertain whether you would be forgiven, if you did not know God would receive and pardon you in case you should repent, would this make any difference as to your duty? Ought you not to repent, whether you are pardoned or not? If you have been doing wrong, ought you not to leave it off, and go to doing right? If a child should run away from his parents' house, and be guilty of many acts of disobedience, ought he not to return and become obedient, even if no reward should be offered to him? Would it be right for this child to insist on being *paid* for returning to his duty? Surely not. You can see in this case, that the child ought to return immediately and obey his parents, whether he expected their pardon or not. He ought to do his own duty, and then let his parents do as they please. So in the case of repentance towards God. You ought to repent, because it is your

duty, whether you are pardoned or not. You
have done wrong, and disobeyed God ; now you
ought to do right, and obey God, whether he
forgives or punishes you. If one should pro-
fess to repent, when he did it only to get a
pardon, and not because he was sorry that he
had done wrong and was resolved to forsake the
ways of sin, it would not be true repentance.
His pretended repentance would be for the sake
of the reward, not on account of his guilt. God
cannot accept this. It would not be repenting.

The Prodigal, when he resolved to go to his
father, did not know that he should be received.
He did not know that his father would own
him, and let him come into his house. Yet he
resolved to do his *duty*. Indeed, he did not expect his father would receive him as a *son ;*
all he thought of asking, was a place as a *hired
servant.* Still, he was not certain that his
father would receive him, even in that humble
station. But he resolved to go; he determined
to return to his duty, whether he should be
admitted into the house or not. Thus he
showed that he was humble, and sorry for his
sins, and truly repented. His father, it is true,
was better to him than he expected. He re-

ceived him as his *son*. He clothed him with
" the best robe, and put a ring on his hands,
and shoes on his feet." He also ordered the
" fatted calf" to be killed, and made a joyful
feast on the occasion. But the humbled Prodigal did not go home expecting to be received
in this splendid manner. He would have gone
even if he had known that no robe, or ring, or
shoes would have been given him. He had
done wrong, and now he was resolved to do
right. He had disobeyed his father, and now
he determined to return and obey him, though
he should be obliged to take the meanest place
in the household.

This was the right kind of repentance. It
was of that kind mentioned in the Scriptures,
when it speaks of a repentance " that needeth
not to be repented of." I love to write about
this repentance of the Prodigal Son; and I
hope my young reader loves to read and think
about it. I wish you to see, in view of this
example, that you ought to repent of your sins
against God, if he had not promised to forgive
you. If you had no hope of pardon, it would
make no difference as to your duty. You ought
to repent and obey God, all the rest of your

life, even if you knew that God would punish
you for ever for your past sins. Having done
wrong, you ought to repent and do right,
whether any good shall come to you or not.
As you are a sinner against God, you ought to
repent and cease from sinning, whether your
repentance is of any advantage to yourself or
not. It depends on the will of God whether
you have a pardon. Your repentance cannot
deserve a pardon. It cannot of itself lay God
under any obligation to forgive you. It is only
doing your duty. It is not the giving of something valuable to God, for which he is bound
to *pay* you. I fear that many persons have
this wrong notion about repentance, that it is
a kind of *paying* for pardon, a kind of *buying*
forgiveness. But surely no person can truly
repent while he has this idea in his mind.
Pardon is the *free gift* of God, not a benefit
purchased by repentance. And if you truly
repent, it must be in view of your sins and
great guilt, not in view of an expected pardon.

It is indeed a precious truth, that God has
promised to forgive you, if you sincerely repent.
But why has he made this promise? Because

the law which sinners have broken. When
God pardons a repenting sinner, he does it *for
Christ's sake*, and not because repentance de·
serves a reward. God has forgiven thousands
of penitent sinners, and he will still forgive all
who truly repent—not because repentance ought
to be *paid for*, but because Jesus died for sinners, and God is merciful. Suppose that God
had never promised to pardon you, if you should
repent—suppose it was uncertain whether you
should be forgiven or not; would this alter your
duty about repenting? Would it make
it right for you to do wrong? Certainly not.
It is your duty to repent, whether God will
pardon you or not. You have done wrong, you
have sinned against God. And now, if you
refuse to repent, you continue to do wrong,
and go on increasing your wickedness and guilt.
This, your own conscience tells you cannot be
right; and therefore it is plain that you ought
to repent and cease to do evil, though no pardon should be granted for your past sins.

Look again at the Prodigal. See him re-
solving to return to his father's house, when
he did not know that his father would receive
him. See him sorrowing for his evil conduct,

and returning to his duty, not knowing what
would be the result, and not at all expecting
to be received into his father's family as a son.
It was not the hope of reward that led him to
repent, but a sense of his guilt, and a desire to
leave the ways of disobedience and sin. This
is the kind of repentance which I wish my
young reader to have. I want you to grieve
on account of your sins against God, and turn
to him with all your heart, and serve him with
a willing mind. And I want you should feel
and do thus because it is right that you should,
and because it is wrong to feel and do other-
wise, and not simply because you hope God
will pardon you. Do your own duty, and let
God do as he sees best. No doubt you will be
forgiven if you repent. But your repentance
must be in view of your sins, and not in view
of an expected pardon.

And now, my young reader, think, I beseech
you, how you have wandered away from your
heavenly Father. Think how you have broken
his laws and abused his goodness. Think of
your wicked feelings and bad conduct. Think
of your going after foolish and sinful pleasures,
and of your neglecting the holy ways of God's

commandments. And think how vile, unholy, polluted, and sinful you are in the sight of God. Have you thought of these things? Do you *now* think of them? If you think as you ought to do, you will appear vile in your own sight. You will see and feel that you are *exceedingly sinful.* And what will you do? Will you remain in this lost, disobedient, and dangerous state? Will you stay away from God *and perish with hunger, and die in your sins?*

The Prodigal, when he saw his lost and miserable condition, said, "I will arise and go to my father." Go, my young reader, and do likewise. Arise, and go to your heavenly Father. Humble yourself before God. Confess your sins before him. Say you have no excuse for your disobedience and guilt. Cast all the blame on yourself. Be grieved for the wickedness of your heart, and beg of God to help you to forsake the ways of sin, and serve him. If you do this with an honest heart, if you are truly sorry for your sins, and forsake them, trusting alone in Christ to save you, if you do all that you know you ought to do, then you have true repentance, and you will be saved.

FAITH

EXPLAINED TO THE UNDERSTANDING
OF THE YOUNG

CHARLES WALKER

ADVERTISEMENT

In this work the author has found it difficult to preserve as much simplicity of language, and to adapt it as clearly to the understanding of children as he desired. It is hoped, however, that it will be intelligible to the greater part of those for whom it was written. Many of the best instructed children between the ages of six and ten will, it is believed, find little difficulty in understanding the language and comprehending the thoughts of this book. And it is hoped there are few between ten and fifteen years of age who will not understand it with ease. But though the work was principally intended for children of the ages here specified, yet the writer hopes that many *youth* will read it, and that they will, by the blessing of God, derive everlasting benefit from its pages.

CONTENTS.

CHAPTER I.

OBJECT OF THE BOOK.

CHAPTER II.

EXAMPLES.

CHAPTER III.

ABEL, ENOCH, AND NOAH.

CHAPTER IV.

ABRAHAM.

CHAPTER V.

MOSES.

CHAPTER VI.

DANIEL AND HIS THREE FRIENDS.

CONCLUSION.

FAITH,

EXPLAINED TO THE UNDERSTANDING

OF

THE YOUNG

CHAPTER I.

OBJECT OF THE BOOK—EXPLANATION OF FAITH.

My young Reader—This little book is about *faith*. It is written to assist you in under-standing what faith is, and to aid you in obtaining it. The writer speaks to you as a friend; will you listen to what he says? Will you give your own mind to the study of this important subject? If you will do so earnestly, you may become wise unto salvation. Of persons of your age, God says in the Scriptures, "Those that seek me early shall find me."

You know that there is much said in the Bible about *faith*. You know that every person must have faith, or he cannot be good and happy. The Bible says, " Without faith it is impossible to please God." If then you hope to please God, and to have his blessing, and to dwell in his presence when you leave this world, you must have faith. So you see it is of the utmost importance that you should know *what faith is*. It is the object of this little book to show you what it is, and to urge you to have it, that you may please God and be happy.

You know that the Holy Bible is the word of God. You know that in the Bible God speaks to us, and tells us about many things which we should never have known, if they had not been told us in that holy book. You know that God speaks to us in the Bible about himself; he tells us who he is, where he dwells, what he has done, and what he will do. God tells us, also, what *we* are ourselves, what we have done, and what we must do, if we would please him. He tells us, too, about another world, a state of being beyond the grave—a place of happiness for the righteous, and a place of misery for the wicked. God tells us, further, about Jesus Christ, who came into the world and died to save sinners ; and that they who believe in Christ shall *be saved,* and that

they who believe not shall *be damned.* All
this, and very much more, God makes known
to us in the Bible.

Now I am ready to tell you what *faith* is :
it is *so believing what God has said, as to do
what he has commanded.* Do you understand
this? I want you should understand it, and
will, therefore, express it in a little different
language. *Faith is believing what God has
said, in such a manner as will lead you to do
what he has bidden.* This is a definition in
general terms. And faith, in this sense, is
applicable to all things that God has said in
the Bible. It regards all that he has said of
himself, of his government, and of his Son
Jesus Christ. It has respect to whatever God
has commanded, and whatever he has forbidden. But more particularly, *Christian* faith,
or that faith by which *a sinner is saved,* may
be explained in this manner : *It is that belief
or trust in Jesus Christ, which will lead us to
rely on him alone for salvation—to commit
our souls, ourselves, our all to him as the only
Saviour, and to obey his commandments.*

It is not enough to say that you believe the
Bible, or to think that you believe it, if you do

not obey it. It is not *faith*, to have a kind of general belief that the Bible is the word of God, and that it is all true. Many have this kind of belief, who have no true faith. If a man has true faith, he will not only believe what God has said in the Bible, but he will *act* as if he believed it. Nor is it enough to say that you believe Christ to be the only Saviour, if you do not follow him. It is not faith in Christ merely to acknowledge him as the only Redeemer. Thousands have this kind of belief, who are utterly destitute of true faith. You will *obey* the Saviour, if you have true faith in him. In the language of Jesus himself, you will *deny yourself, and take up the cross and follow him.*

What I have now said will show my young reader what true faith is, as clearly as I can do it in a few words. But I hope to make the subject much plainer, before I close this book. And I shall try to do it by pointing you to the example of many good men who had faith, and who showed what their faith was by what they did.

But before I proceed to notice these examples, I have several things to say. The great object of the Christian's faith is the Lord Jesus

Christ. He is the only Saviour. And the only way in which we can be saved, is *by faith* in him. The Bible says, " Believe in the Lord Jesus Christ, and thou shalt be saved." And it says also, " He that believeth not, shall be damned." It is plain, therefore, that our salvation depends on our having true faith in the Saviour.

Now, you know what God has told us in the holy Scriptures about his Son. You remember what the Bible says about the birth, life, and death of Jesus. Though he dwelt in heaven, and " was with God, and was God," yet he came into this world, and became a man. He was born of the virgin Mary. He grew up like other children. " He increased in wisdom and stature, and in favor with God and man." When he was thirty years old, he began his ministry. He preached that all men must repent and believe in him, or they can never enter the kingdom of heaven. He performed a great many wonderful miracles, which proved that God was with him, and that he " worked the works of God." His life was entirely holy, free from all manner of sin. His example was perfectly good, and he urged all men to be like himself. His teaching was wise and good Even his enemies said, "Never man spake like this man." He told all about the duties which mankind owe to each other, and to God. He earnestly besought all people to become his disciples and friends, telling them if they would follow him, they should be happy for ever, and if they would not, they must be eternally miserable. Such were the things that Jesus taught, and in this manner he labored to save men. And at last he permitted himself to be taken and crucified by wicked men, that, by his death, he might make an atonement for the sins of the world, and prepare a way that all sinners, who repent and believe in him, might be saved and be happy in heaven for ever. After his death, he arose from the grave, appeared alive to his disciples, told them to "go into all the world, and preach the Gospel to every creature;" and then he ascended into heaven in the sight of many of his friends, and there "he ever liveth to make intercession for us."

This is a short account of what the Bible informs us concerning the Saviour. Now God requires that we should *believe* this, and *so* believe it that it will rule our conduct, and make us the followers and disciples of Jesus Christ. This is *faith* in Jesus Christ; and nothing else *is* true faith in him. It is not enough for you to say that you do not dispute or deny what God says concerning his Son. It is not enough for you to say that you believe the scripture account of the Saviour. If your belief is not of that kind which will govern your *actions*, if it does not lead you to do as the Saviour bids you, if it does not make you his friend and disciple, it is not true faith in him.

Now, my young reader, if you have read attentively and understood what you have read, you see that when you have true faith in Christ, you will trust yourself in his hands; you will look to him alone for salvation; you will obey his commands, and strive to be like him. Your belief in Jesus, your faith in him, will control your conduct: it will lead you to do as Jesus bids you; it will make you a friend of the Saviour, and you will be a Christian indeed. This is the faith that God speaks of in the Bible, and it is the only kind of faith that he will accept, or that will prepare the soul for heaven. If you would have this faith, you must study the Bible very attentively, you

must earnestly desire to know all that God
has said; and you must pray much that God
would help you to understand and do his will,
and that he would give you the faith which
all true Christians have.

Consider, my young friend, why you yourself need faith. It is because you are a sinner.
Did you ever seriously think of this? *You are
a sinner.* You have naturally a wicked heart,
have disobeyed God, and come into condemnation. The Bible says, "He that believeth not,
is condemned already." The only way to escape this condemnation is by faith in Christ.
He came to save sinners. He says, "The Son
of man came to seek and to save that which
was lost." You are a *lost* one. You have wandered away from duty and from God, and you
will perish for ever, if you are not saved by
Jesus Christ. And this is the reason why you
need faith in him. If you have it not, you
will be lost eternally. O think of this—*feel*
it; and then cast yourself, with deep repentance, at the Saviour's feet, and cry, "Lord,
save me, or I perish." If you do this sincerely,
trusting in him alone, it will be exercising faith
in him, and you will be pardoned and saved.

CHAPTER II.

EXAMPLES.

I WILL now attempt to show you what faith is, by some familiar examples. Suppose, then, that your father should tell you, that in a distant field, under a certain stone, there is a large sum of money, and that if you will go and get it, you shall have it for your own. Knowing your father to be a man of truth, and that he means what he says, you will believe what he has told you. You may not understand how he happens to know about it, and he may not explain the matter to you; but if he tells you that he does know, and that if you will go where he directs, you will find the money, you will *believe* him. But how, in this case, will you show your belief? How will it influence you? The answer is plain: you will go immediately to the place that your father pointed out, and search for the prize, find it, and bring it home. If you should not move, if what your father told you should have no effect upon you, it would be plain that you did not believe what he said; for if you *believed* him, you would set out at once to get the prize.

Now, to apply this : God, your heavenly Father, has told you of heaven, where you may enjoy perfect happiness, and have every thing that your heart shall desire, when you arrive there. He has told you, also, about the way that leads to heaven. He says you must repent of sin, believe in Jesus Christ, follow him and obey his commandments, and then you shall not fail of entering into the kingdom of heaven. And God has further told you, that if you do not go in the way he has pointed out, if you do not obey him and follow the Saviour, you shall be cast down to hell, and be miserable for ever. All these things, which are as important to you as your soul's happiness, God has plainly revealed in the Bible. Now, if you believe what he has said, will it not deeply affect your mind? And if you truly believe the sayings of God on this subject, what will you do? Will you remain careless, and do nothing? Certainly not. You will *seek to enter the strait and narrow way that leadeth unto life.* You will be in earnest in trying to secure the salvation of your soul. Not daring to remain in a state of impenitence and danger, you will repent, and come to the Lord Jesus Christ for pardon and help.

Depending on the Saviour, you will perform all those duties which God has commanded. You will "seek first the kingdom of God and his righteousness," trusting in the promise that all things necessary "shall be added unto you." Thus will you do, and do immediately, if you truly believe what God has said in his holy word.

But if you do none of these things, if you remain careless and unconcerned about your present character and future state, if you are not *moved* by what God tells you in the Bible, can it be that you truly believe what he has said? No, certainly not. You see plainly that your belief is not of the right kind. It does not move you. It does not govern your actions. It is only a *dead* faith, such as the apostle James speaks of when he says, " Faith, if it hath not works, is dead, being alone." " For as the body without the spirit is dead, so faith without works is dead also."

One thing very important to a true idea of faith, is *trust* in God. To show you what this means, I will bring another example. The Rev. Richard Cecil, an English clergyman, took the following method to give his daughter

an idea of faith, when she was very young.
He wished to teach her what it is *to trust in
God*, which is the very essence of true faith.
He says, " My little daughter was playing one
day with a few beads, which seemed to delight
her wonderfully. Her whole soul seemed to
be absorbed in her beads. I said, ' My dear,
you have some pretty beads there.' ' Yes, papa.'
' And you seem to be vastly pleased with them.'
' Yes, papa.' ' Well now, throw them into the
fire.' The tears started into her eyes. She
looked earnestly at me, as though she ought to
have a reason for such a cruel sacrifice. ' Well,
my dear, do as you please ; but you know I
never told you to do any thing which I did not
think would be good for you.' She looked at
me a few moments longer, and then summon-
ing up all her fortitude, her breast heaving
with the effort, she dashed them into the fire.
' Well,' said I, ' there let them lie ; you shall
hear more about them at another time, but say
no more about them now.' Some days after, I
bought her a box full of larger beads, and toys
of the same kind. When I returned home, I
opened the treasure, and set it before her ; she
burst into tears with joy. ' Those, my child,'

said I, 'are yours, because you believed me, when I told you it would be better for you to throw those two or three paltry beads into the fire. Now, that has brought you this treasure. But now, my dear, remember, as long as you live, what *faith* is. I did all this to teach you the meaning of FAITH. You threw your beads away when I bade you, because you had faith in me that I never advised you but for your good. Put the same trust in God. Believe every thing that he says in his word. Whether you understand it or not, have faith in him that he means your good.' "

This example, my young reader, shows you, in a very striking manner, the nature of true faith. You will, I think, always remember it. By looking at it, you can, at all times, see what it is *to trust in God.* When God commands you to throw away your vain trifles, which draw away your heart from him, you know that he intends your own good; and that if you obey him, you will have something better than what you give up. When God commands you, as he does in the Bible, "Love not the world, nor the things of the world," he will, if you obey him, give you the better things of

heaven. When he urges you to give up every
improper pleasure, and to forsake the vanities
of a wicked world, if you cheerfully comply,
though it may cost you some present struggles
and pain, you shall, in the end, know that what
God required was for your own good.   In the
Bible, God commands you to forsake the ways
of sinful pleasure, to avoid the company and
example of the wicked, to give up your own
will, and to deny yourself, and take up the
cross, and follow Christ.   Perhaps you may
sometimes think, that to do so would make
you unhappy. But remember, that God never
calls upon you to do any thing but what will
be for your own good.   Trust in him—*throw
your beads into the fire*—give up your worldly
desires, and obey the voice of the Lord.   You
will find, at last, that this is the best way, that
it is the only way to true happiness, and that
the Lord will ever take care of those who put
their *trust* in him.   Long ago the psalmist
said, and he said it too from his own experi-
ence, " O Lord, blessed is the man that trust-
eth in thee."

Mr. Cecil's little daughter thought at first,
that if she should obey her father, and throw

her playthings into the fire, she should have nothing to amuse herself with, and that she should be very unhappy. And though she knew that her father never told her to do any thing except it was best that she should do it, yet it cost her a painful struggle to give up present pleasure, and trust in him for a future and unknown good. But she did it, and found a rich reward. So, many young persons think, that if they should obey God, and give up their sinful amusements and worldly desires, and should become serious and pious, and attend to all the duties of religion, they should be unhappy. But it is not so. God never commands you to do any thing but what is for your own benefit. Try it, and see. Though it may seem hard for you to forsake the way that leads you to sin, to give up your own will and become the servant of Jesus Christ, yet, if you will do it, if you will obey God and trust in him, you shall be more happy in this world than ever you have been, and you shall be for ever happy in the world to come.

You must remember, however, that you are not to expect to *buy* the favor of God, by giving up your sinful pleasures. You do not *pay* him for his blessings, by forsaking the ways of sin. God's favors are *gifts;* you cannot purchase them by what you do. When he commands you to give up a vain amusement, a sinful pleasure, or your own will, you must do it *because* he commands it. His commands are right and good, and you should obey them cheerfully, whether he bestow more blessings on you or not. Do his will, obey his commands, and then leave the consequences to his care. This is *trusting in him.* This is *faith.*

CHAPTER III.

ABEL, ENOCH, AND NOAH.

I WILL now turn to the Bible, and give my young readers a number of examples, out of that holy book, of good men who had faith. By looking at these examples, you will be able to see what faith is, and how it influences the feelings and conduct of those who have it.

In the eleventh chapter of the epistle to the Hebrews, the apostle Paul mentions a large number of men who lived in ancient times, and who all "obtained a good report *through faith.*" I will tell you something of several of these good men, taking them in the order in which the apostle mentions them.

The first in the order is ABEL. The apostle says, "*By faith* Abel offered unto God a more excellent sacrifice than Cain, by which he obtained witness that he was righteous, God testifying of his gifts ; and by it, he being dead, yet speaketh." Now, if you will turn to the fourth chapter of Genesis, you will find the account to which the apostle refers. Cain and Abel were brothers, and the sons of Adam and

Eve. But though they were brothers, they were very different from each other. One was a very good man, and the other a very bad man. One had *faith*, the other had not. Cain was a tiller of the ground; that is, he was a husbandman, or farmer. Abel was a keeper of sheep. The Bible says, "In process of time it came to pass, that Cain brought of the fruit of the ground an offering unto the Lord. And Abel, he also brought of the firstlings of his flock, and of the fat thereof. And the Lord had respect unto Abel, and to his offering; but unto Cain, and to his offering, he had not respect. And Cain was very wroth, and his countenance fell. And the Lord said unto Cain, Why art thou wroth? and why is thy countenance fallen? If thou doest well, shalt thou not be accepted? and if thou doest not well, sin lieth at the door. And Cain talked with Abel his brother; and it came to pass when they were in the field, that Cain rose up against Abel his brother, and slew him."

This wicked deed of Cain placed him first on the list of murderers, and his name has always been covered with reproach. God was displeased with him. and put a curse upon him ; and he was doomed to be *a fugitive and a vagabond on the earth.*

And now my young reader will desire to know why God "had respect to," or accepted Abel's offering, and did not accept Cain's. The reason is made known to us by the apostle, in the words before mentioned : " By *faith* Abel offered unto God a more excellent sacrifice than Cain." Abel had faith, and Cain had not : this made the difference between them. Abel truly believed what God said, trusted in him, and obeyed him. His offering was a kid, or a lamb, and was typical of the sacrifice which Christ, as the Lamb of God, made on Calvary for the sins of men. When Abel brought his offering and presented it, he felt himself to be God's servant, and bound to do his will. He gave up *himself* to the Lord ; and he brought his offering as a proof that he did so, and that he stood ready to do whatever God should command him to do. This was a state of mind pleasing to God, and thus he accepted Abel and his offering.

Cain did not give up his own will, and submit himself to God. He had no childlike trust in God, and did not feel willing to take the place of a servant, and do God's will. He brought an offering of the fruits of the earth having no reference to Christ's atoning sacrifice. He was proud and stubborn; he had the spirit of a rebel, and God would not accept him, nor receive the offering from his hands.

What a difference there was between these two brothers! Though both of them professed to worship God, yet one did it with a humble, believing, and childlike spirit; while the other came with a proud, worldly, and rebellious temper. The one, when he presented his offering, presented also *himself*, to be a servant of God, and obey all his commandments; the other brought his offering, but his heart was not with it, and his hand was not ready to do the will of God. The one had *faith;* the other had not. This made the difference between them. And then one became a murderer, and the other the victim of a brother's rage. Abel was accepted, Cain was rejected. The one is happy with God in heaven; the other, so far as we know, is in the pit of eternal misery.

From this example, my young reader, you see how important it is to have faith. Without it, you cannot serve God aright, and cannot be accepted by him. You may learn, also, in the case of Abel, what true faith is, and what it will do. From the sad case of Cain, also, you may learn how wicked a person *may* become, and what dreadful deeds he *may* commit, if he lives without faith, and permits his angry passions to rage against any of his fellow-creatures. Let it be a warning to you : go to God in humble prayer, and ask him to give you that faith which will preserve you from evil ways, and make you holy and happy for ever.

The next example mentioned by the apostle, in the eleventh chapter of Hebrews, is that of ENOCH. He says, "*By faith* Enoch was translated, that he should not see death; and was not found, because God had translated him: for before his translation he had this testimony, that he pleased God." *Translated* means that he was taken up into heaven; *not see death* means that he did not die. Here then was a good man, who did not die, but God took him at once into heaven. Before he was taken up, he pleased God by his pious and holy life. And why was he so remarkable for his piety and

holiness? Why was God so much pleased with
him? Why did he have so much proof that
God loved him? And why was he taken away
from the evils of this life, without feeling the
pains of death, and received into the presence
of God, and the joys of heaven? The apostle
gives the answer: "By *faith* Enoch was translated." It was his *faith* which made him so
good a man. It was his trust in God, his doing
the will of God, and his living here with his
thoughts and heart fixed on heaven, that so
pleased God that he took him to himself.

In Gen. 5 : 24, you may find the history of
the event to which the apostle refers: "And
Enoch walked with God; and he was not, for
God took him." This is a short account, but
there is much meaning in it. He *walked with
God;* that is, he felt and acted as if God were
present with him. His faith was so strong, that
it brought God and eternal things constantly
before his mind. He felt that God was around
him, and with him. With the eye of faith he
constantly beheld his Maker, and walked in the
path of obedience all his days. You know the
Bible speaks of wicked men as living "*without* God in the world." They have no sense of

his presence. They forgot that he notices their conduct. They live and act as if there were no God; for "they do not like to retain God in their knowledge." But Enoch walked *with* God. He felt that the eye of God was upon him, and his constant aim was to do the things that would please God.

Again, the account says, "He was not, for God took him;" that is, he could not be found in the world, for God had taken him to heaven. Perhaps he was alone, when God translated him. Perhaps no one was with him, to see him go up into heaven. When the prophet Elijah was taken up to heaven, Elisha saw him go, and he could tell what he had seen, so that every body would know that Elijah had gone, without dying, to the heavenly world. But if no one saw Enoch ascend to heaven, it would not be known where he was. It might never have been known where he was, if God had not told us. But God has told us. In the Old Testament we read, " He was not, for God took him;" and in the New Testament it is said, " By faith Enoch was translated, that he should not see death."

In this example, my young reader, you see

what faith is. It is that state of mind in which
a man feels that God is with him, and notices
all his feelings and conduct. It is a full and
impressive belief that God sees you at all
times, and that he will call you to an account
for all that you think, and say, and do. You
see, also, in this example, the effects of faith.
It will lead you, if you have it, to walk with
God, to do the things that please him, to obey
his laws, and engage in his service. And
though you have no reason to expect that you
shall be translated to heaven without dying, as
Enoch was; yet, if you have true faith, your
soul will go upward to dwell with God, when
you die, and you will be happy in his presence
for ever.

Let us look a little longer at the case of
Enoch. It was a remarkable case. He was
a man like other men. He was, by nature, a
sinner, and dwelt among sinners. But he repented of sin, and turned to the Lord. If you
had lived at that time, you might not have
seen any difference, in outward appearance,
between him and other men. You might have
seen him attending to the business of this
world, like his neighbors. But while his hands

were engaged in the affairs of this life, his heart was set on things above. While others laid up their treasures on earth, he laid up his treasures in heaven. While others walked in the broad way that leadeth to death, he walked with God. He kept eternal things constantly before his mind. He thought of God, and heaven, and hell, and acted as though he could see them all. He prayed unto God, and watched against sin. He desired to be entirely holy, and by constant prayer and watchfulness assisted by the Spirit of God, he did become so holy that God took him away from this world into heaven. And all this was because he had *faith*.

Now I hope that every reader of this little book will "obtain like precious faith." I hope that you will think so much and so earnestly about what God has told you in the Bible, that you will fully believe it all, and feel and act as you should do. If you believe, with all your heart, what the Bible says about God, and Christ, and heaven, and hell, and about your own duty, that will be faith, and you will then do the things that are pleasing to God.

NOAH is the next example of faith mentioned by the apostle. You remember that Noah and his family were preserved alive, when all the other people of the world were drowned by a flood of waters. You remember, too, by what means he was preserved; that he built a large ark, or vessel, and rode safely in it on the surface of the flood which drowned a world. The apostle tells us why the ark was built, and why the man and his family were saved. It was because he had *faith*—because he believed what God said. The language is this: "*By faith* Noah, being warned of God of things not seen as yet, moved with fear, prepared an ark to the saving of his house, by the which he condemned the world, and became heir of the righteousness which is by faith."

Long before the flood came, God warned men that it was coming. Noah believed the warning, and set himself to prepare for the event. When God told him that he could no longer bear with the wickedness of men, and that the world was so full of sin that he was determined to sweep the whole race of sinners from the face of the earth, Noah had faith in the word of the Lord, and believed he would do as he said. But we do not learn that there were any others among all the people, who believed the divine threatening. All the rest seemed to be utterly careless about the matter. They lived thoughtlessly, and pursued vain and wicked courses as before. Not so with Noah. He, " being warned of God, was moved with fear." He fully believed that the flood would come, and fearing lest himself and his family should be involved in the common ruin, he began at once, as God directed him, to build the ark. By doing so, he showed his faith; and his conduct, as the Bible says, " condemned the world ;" that is, it was a rebuke to the wicked men of that time, who would not believe what God said.

It was many years after the warning was given, before the flood came. Noah, the Bible says, was " a preacher of righteousness." He doubtless preached to his neighbors, and to all who heard his voice, the great truths which God had spoken. He told them their wickedness, and their great guilt in the sight of God. But they cared not for his sayings. He warned them of their danger, told them that a flood was coming, and that a more awful punishment than to be drowned in a flood of waters, would come upon them in another world, if they did not repent. But they did not regard his warnings. The truth was, they had no faith, they did not believe what Noah said, they did not believe what God said. No threatenings alarmed them. No warnings moved them. No kind invitations, no affectionate entreaties had any effect on their minds. They were just like the careless and thoughtless sinners who live in the world now. Ministers preach to them, and Christian friends entreat them, but they will not repent, they will not believe, and become Christians. O, how hard and wicked are the hearts of sinners! And you, my young reader, if you will not regard what God says in the Bible, if you will not mind what the minister of the gospel says, if you will not repent, and have faith, and be a disciple of Christ, when your friends urge you to do it, you are like the sinners that lived in the days of Noah. They would not hear the warnings of God, and turn unto him, and you will not. Are you not, then, like them? O, be like them no longer. Hear the warning now, and fly to Jesus Christ, who is the true ark of safety.

The building of the ark, as well as Noah's preaching, should have awakened the attention of the people of those days. This work was a constant warning to them, and they ought to have been alarmed by it, and to have repented, and turned unto the Lord. Noah, by all the labor he performed in building that great vessel, showed the strength of his faith, and his firm belief that the flood would come. His neighbors, when they saw him, with so much toil and expense, preparing an ark for the saving of his house, ought to have inquired whether they were not in danger. They, no doubt, saw him engaged in the work. They knew him to be a good man, and his conduct was abundant proof to them that he sincerely believed a flood was coming. Why, then, did they not feel alarmed? Why did they not prepare for the coming of the awful judgment? Alas, it was because they were unbelieving and wicked. They loved their sinful pleasures and worldly pursuits, and after them they would go. The Saviour says, "They were eating and drinking, marrying and giving in marriage, until the day that Noe entered into the ark, and knew not until the flood came and took them

all away." What folly! What madness! What
slaves they were to sin!

But such conduct was very much like the
conduct of sinners at the present day. Even
now, under the clear light of the blessed gospel, careless sinners can see their pious friend
or neighbor earnestly preparing himself for the
judgment of the great day, and remain thoughtless and unconcerned themselves. They can
see the Christian watching and praying and
denying himself, and laying up his treasure in
heaven, and yet feel no alarm at their own
dreadful danger. I fear that some who read
this little book, are thus heedless and impenitent. How is it with you, young reader?
When you see your father or mother, or some
Christian neighbor, preparing for death and
judgment, are you not careless? Does it alarm
you any to see others preparing an ark for
the saving of their souls, while you have
none? While others are afraid to disobey God
and live without religion, do not you disobey
him and live carelessly, without fear? How
much this looks like the conduct of those who
lived in the time of Noah. Let me entreat
you to live in this careless and dangerous

state no longer. Strive to enter into the ark of safety.

When the ark was done, Noah and his wife, his three sons and their wives, entered into it. And the Bible says, " The Lord shut him in." Now they were safe, and all the rest of the world were shut out. It was now too late for any to ask to be admitted into the ark. All without must perish. Soon the rain began to descend in torrents. " The windows of heaven were opened, and the fountains of the great deep were broken up." Now, we may suppose, many wanted to be received into the ark. They ran to it, in hopes that the door would be opened. Perhaps they cried aloud unto Noah, and earnestly besought him to let them in. But this could not be. The Lord had shut him in, and, by doing so, had shut all others out. It was too late to seek refuge there. As the vallies became filled with water, these frightened sinners ran to the hills and mountains. But they could not be safe there. The waters continued to rise. The lowest hills were covered first, and the men, women, and children who had collected there, were drowned. Then the higher hills, and at last the highest mountains were covered with the waters. The miserable people struggled a little while in the waves, and then sunk to the bottom. All were drowned. Not one of all that wicked race remained alive. The Lord was offended with them; he made all the earth one vast ocean, and they all perished. O, what an awful scene was this! Who will not fear the judgments of the Lord? Who will not tremble, when he comes to take vengeance on his enemies?

But amidst all this desolation and death, Noah and his family were safe. The ark bore them up on the top of the flood, and God preserved them. Soon the waters began to abate. The ark rested on mount Ararat. In a few days the dry land began to appear. And shortly after, the waters having departed and the ground having become dry, Noah and his family came forth out of the ark. They found themselves alone on the earth, and began the world anew.

In this example, my young reader sees what *faith* is, and what it does. Noah owed his safety, under God, to his faith. He believed God, he believed what God said respecting the coming flood, and he *acted* as though he believed it. This was true faith. And if you, my reader, will believe God, if you will fully believe what God says in the Bible, what he says about himself and about his laws, what he says about the Saviour and about yourself, what he says about eternity, heaven and hell, and your own duty—if you will *fully believe* all these things, *and act as though you believed them*, you will have faith. Do this, and God will own you as a child. The Saviour will acknowledge you as his disciple. You will be safe from all the floods of wrath that are coming upon the ungodly. In the ark of salvation you will abide here, and in heaven shall you dwell for ever.

CHAPTER IV.

ABRAHAM.

FOLLOWING the order of the apostle in the eleventh chapter of the epistle to the Hebrews, the next example of faith mentioned, is that of ABRAHAM. He was truly a striking example. When we read his history, as it is written in the Bible, we find that, in many instances, he showed a remarkably strong and active faith. The most remarkable instance was that when he offered up his son Isaac, which we cannot read, without being filled with wonder at his cheerful obedience and steady trust in God. He would do any thing that God commanded him to do, whatever it might be ; and so strong was his faith and confidence in God, that he is justly called *the father of the faithful.*

The apostle says, "*By faith* Abraham, when he was called to go out into a place which he should after receive for an inheritance, obeyed ; and he went out, not knowing whither he went." Abraham knew that God never gave a command without having wise reasons for it ; and though he might not be able to see why the command was given, yet he knew

that it was best for him to obey it. He was
fully satisfied, that whatever God commanded
was right, and that if he obeyed, God would
take care of him. This was faith. It might
have been painful to the feelings of Abraham,
to leave his own country and his father's house,
and go to an unknown country. He was, no
doubt, strongly attached to his friends, and to
the place where he was born, and to break away
from them may have cost him a severe struggle.
But God had commanded it, and that was
enough. He did not hesitate or delay, but went
off immediately, "not knowing whither he
went."

You may find the account of God's command,
and of Abraham's going forth, in the twelfth
chapter of Genesis. His name was then called Abram; it was afterwards changed to Abraham. "Now the Lord had said to Abram, Get
thee out of thy country, and from thy kindred,
and from thy father's house, unto a land that
I will show thee." At that time, the world
was full of idolatry. The people had forgotten
God, and made themselves idols to worship, and
they were generally wicked and corrupt in the
sight of God. True religion was almost ban-

ished from the earth. There was, indeed, some
piety in the family to which Abram belonged,
and he himself was truly pious, and the friend
of God. But the people generally were so sunk
in sin and pollution, that God saw it needful
to separate Abram from the rest of mankind,
lest his family, if not himself, should become
as wicked and corrupt as others. This was
probably the reason why God told Abram to
leave his country and his father's house. And
for the same reason he caused Abram to remove
from place to place during his whole life, that
he might not live long enough in one place, to
permit his family to mingle with the people
that lived about them. God told Abram that
he would give his children all the country of
Canaan, now called Palestine, but he did not let
Abram have any one place in the land. Abram
built no houses, but dwelt in tents, and removed
from place to place. In this way, his family
was kept distinct from the people of the land.
Perhaps Abram felt that such a moving life
was not pleasant to him. It gave him much
trouble, and prevented his building a comfort-
able house to dwell in. But God commanded
him to move about in this manner, and that

was enough for Abram. He would do what God said, and thus he showed his faith.

I have spoken of Abram's family, when he had not, as yet, any children of his own. His wife Sarah had no child. But he had many men-servants and maid-servants in his family, and his household became very numerous. At a certain time when Lot, who was the son of Abram's brother, had been taken captive by a large force, Abram armed his servants, three hundred and eighteen in number, and went and released Lot, and all his family. This shows that the company which Abram had about him, and which was called his own family, was very great. He trained up all these to fear and worship God. He built an altar to the Lord wherever they journeyed and pitched their tents. He was the priest or minister of his own large family, and taught them to love and serve God.

It is now time to mention another thing which showed and tried Abram's faith, and which makes known to us what true faith is. God had promised to give to Abram's posterity, that is, to his own children and descendants, the whole land of Canaan. But Abram's wife had no child. How then was God's promise to

be fulfilled? Almost any other man would have
doubted the promise of God, when the fulfil-
ment of it was so long delayed. But Abram
believed it still. He did not know *how* God
would fulfil his promise, but he believed he
would do it. This was faith. After Abram
became very old, God made the promise to him
again, and told him that he should be "the
father of many nations." He also changed
the name of Abram, and called him Abraham,
which means, "father of a great multitude."

At length, when Abraham was ninety-nine
years old, and Sarah his wife ninety, God appeared unto him, and told him that Sarah
should have a son. In such circumstances,
perhaps no one but Abraham would have believed that the promise would be fulfilled. But
Abraham did believe. "He staggered not at
the promise of God through unbelief; but was
strong in faith, giving glory to God; and being
fully persuaded, that what he had promised,
he was able to perform." This is what Paul
says of the matter, Rom. 4 : 20, 21.

This promise was again renewed in such an
interesting manner, that I will relate the story
as it is found in the first part of the eighteenth

chapter of Genesis. "And the Lord appeared
unto him in the plains of Mamre : and he,"
Abraham, "sat in the tent-door in the heat of
the day ; and he lifted up his eyes and looked,
and lo, three men stood by him ; and when he
saw them, he ran to meet them from the tent-
door, and bowed himself towards the ground,
and said, My Lord, if now I have found favor
in thy sight, pass not away, I pray thee, from
thy servant. Let a little water, I pray you,
be fetched, and wash your feet, and rest your-
selves under the tree. And I will fetch a mor-
sel of bread, and comfort ye your hearts ; after
that ye shall pass on ; for therefore are ye come
to your servant. And they said unto him, So
do, as thou hast said. And Abraham hastened
into the tent unto Sarah, and said, Make ready
quickly three measures of fine meal, knead it,
and make cakes upon the hearth. And Abraham ran unto the herd, and fetched a calf ten-
der and good, and gave it to a young man ; and
he hasted to dress it. And he took butter and
milk, and the calf which he had dressed, and
set it before them ; and he stood by them under
the tree, and they did eat. And they said unto
him, Where is Sarah thy wife ? And he said,

Behold, in the tent. And he," the Lord, "said, I will certainly return unto thee according to the time of life; and lo, *Sarah thy wife shall have a son.*"

Thus kind and hospitable was Abraham, and thus was he again cheered with the precious promise that he should have a son. He believed the promise, though as he was now about a hundred years old, it did not appear likely, in man's view, that it would be fulfilled. But Abraham thought that *nothing was too hard for the Lord,* and he trusted in the word of God that he should have a son in his old age. The Lord had said it—this was enough for Abraham. He believed it, and this was faith.

In God's own time the promise was fulfilled. It was delayed till Abraham's strong faith was fully proved and manifested. It was delayed till it was found that his faith was so strong, that, as Paul says, he "against hope believed in hope." Then the blessing came. Sarah bore a son to Abraham, and they called his name Isaac. There was much rejoicing at his birth, and when the child was weaned, Abraham made a great feast for all his household. There was, without doubt, gladness in all the family, for

it was now seen that God would fulfil his promises and never disappoint those who put their
trust in him. It was seen, also, how God might
fulfil all his other promises to Abraham—that
he would make him " the father of many nations ;" that he would give his posterity " all
the land of Canaan ;" and that " all the nations
of the earth" should be blessed in him. These
promises God had made, and it was now seen
how they might all come to pass. Well might
Abraham and all his family rejoice.

After a few years, when this child became
a youth, there was another and more severe
trial made of Abraham's faith. In this trial,
the good man not only shows what faith is, and
proves that he had it; but he shows us, also,
that it is a most powerful principle when it is
fixed deep in the soul. He had such a strong
confidence in God, such a firm belief that it
would be best for him to obey God, whatever
was commanded, that he would do *any thing*
which God told him to do.

The apostle tells us, in the chapter so often
mentioned, " *By faith* Abraham, when he was
tried, offered up Isaac ; and he that had received the promises, offered up his only begotten

son, of whom it was said, that in Isaac shall thy seed be called." The history of the case here brought to view is most extraordinary and affecting. It shows both "the goodness and severity of God" in a striking manner. God requires men to obey him, whether they can see the reason of his commands or not. He gives no command without reason; and he always intends the good of men in all the commands he lays upon them. But they cannot always see why he gives such commands as he sometimes does, and it may be difficult for them, in some cases, to see how their own good is to be promoted by obedience. But, at such times, God requires them to obey, to do their duty, and leave the event with him. This Abraham did, and the history of his offering up Isaac affords, probably, the most striking example of confidence in God which has ever been seen in this world.

You may find the history in the twenty-second chapter of Genesis. It reads in this manner: "And it came to pass after these things, that God did tempt," or try, "Abraham, and said unto him, Abraham; and he said, Behold, here I am. And God said, Take now thy son, thine only son Isaac, whom thou lovest, and get thee into the land of Moriah; and offer him there for a burnt-offering upon one of the mountains which I will tell thee of. And Abraham rose up early in the morning, and saddled his ass, and took two of his young men with him, and Isaac his son, and clave the wood for the burnt-offering, and rose up, and went unto the place of which God had told him. Then on the third day Abraham lifted up his eyes, and saw the place afar off. And Abraham said unto his young men, Abide ye here with the ass, and I and the lad will go yonder and worship, and come again to you. And Abraham took the wood of the burnt-offering, and laid it upon Isaac his son; and he took the fire in his hand and a knife; and they went both of them together. And Isaac spake unto Abraham his father, and said, My father; and he said, Here am I, my son. And he said, Behold the fire and the wood; but where is the lamb for a burnt-offering? And Abraham said, My son, God will provide himself a lamb for a burnt-offering; so they went both of them together. And they came to the place which God had told him of; and Abraham built an altar there, and laid the wood in order; and bound Isaac his son, and laid him on the altar upon the wood. And Abraham stretched forth his hand, and took the knife to slay his son. And the angel of the Lord called unto him out of heaven, and said, Abraham, Abraham. And he said, Here am I. And he said, Lay not thine hand upon the lad, neither do thou any thing unto him; for now I know that thou fearest God, seeing thou hast not withheld thy son, thine only son, from me. And Abraham lifted up his eyes, and looked, and behold, behind him a ram caught in a thicket by his horns; and Abraham went and took the ram, and offered him up for a burnt-offering in the stead of his son."

What a trial, and what a deliverance was here! How calmly and steadfastly Abraham went forward obeying the command of God; and how kindly did God prevent the death of Isaac, as soon as Abraham's faith was tried, and it was found that he would do any thing which God commanded him to do.

In this example we see true faith in its strongest actings. God laid on Abraham a very severe command. He does not commonly give such hard commands; but he had a rea-

son for this. He had a good object in view.
He placed Abraham on this trial for his good,
and for the good of the world, that all men
might see a striking example of faith and obedience. Abraham endured the trial with perfect composure and submission. When the
command came, he did not complain, did not
ask to be excused, but immediately began to
obey it.

We can see how most men would have tried
to excuse themselves from obeying this command. And we can see, too, how Abraham
might have thought and acted if he had been
a different man, and had been disposed to neglect obedience. He might have said, Isaac is
my beloved son; how then shall I take away
his life? It is wrong to kill any human being,
and much more wicked to kill my own son.
Besides, God has promised that *in Isaac shall
my seed be called;* and how can this promise
be fulfilled if Isaac is slain? God has promised, also, to give all this land, wherein I am
a stranger, to my posterity; how will this
promise be kept, if Isaac, my only son, is offered up for a burnt-sacrifice? How will God
make me " the father of many nations," as he

has promised to do; and how will "all nations be blessed" in me, and by my descendants, if the only child I have is cut off? And what will my neighbors think of me and of my religion, if I murder my own child? Or what will Sarah my wife say, if I kill the son of our old age? All these things Abraham might have pleaded as reasons why he should not obey the command of God. But he pleaded none of them. He had not a word to say. God had spoken: Abraham had heard the command; and now he considered that he had nothing to do but to obey.

He did not, at the time, know *how* this command was to be overruled for good. He did not know how his family and neighbors were to be convinced that he had not done wrong. He did not know how the promises of God were to be fulfilled, if Isaac should be sacrificed. But he felt that these things were no concern of his. He believed that God would take care of consequences. He believed that God would, in some way or other, fulfil his promises, though he could not see how it would be done. He fully believed that it would be best for him to obey God. His duty

was obedience, and he could willingly and
cheerfully trust God for what should follow.
He went on, therefore, with steady purpose,
to sacrifice his son. He travelled three days'
journey till he came in sight of the mountain.
Then he left the young men, that they might
not witness the painful scene, and might not in-
terfere to prevent his purpose. Taking Isaac,
and the wood, and the fire, and the knife, he
went up the mountain. Isaac's question must
have been very trying to his feelings: "My father, behold the wood and the fire; but where
is the lamb for a burnt-offering?" Abraham's
answer was just such an answer as such a
man would give: "My son, God will provide
himself a lamb for a burnt-offering." If Isaac
was to be sacrificed, God had provided *him*
for the lamb; and if any thing was offered in
his stead, God must provide it. Abraham was
going to obey God; this he felt was all he had
to do in the solemn transaction. It is not
probable that he expected any other lamb to be
provided in the place of his son. He thought
that Isaac was the lamb, and must die. It
appears so, from what the apostle says in Heb.
11 : 19, that Abraham, when he was about to

sacrifice Isaac, "accounted that God was able to
raise him up even from the dead:" another proof
of his trust in God, and of his strong faith.

Having come to the top of the mountain,
Abraham gathered the stones together for the
altar.   In this work, Isaac, no doubt, assisted
him.   He then built the altar, and laid the
wood upon it.   And now the moment of the
severest trial came.   And did Abraham hesitate?   No.   He loved his son, and all the ten-
der feelings of a father dwelt in his bosom.
But God had bidden ; and did Abraham now
beg to be excused from the painful deed?   No.
He took hold of Isaac with a steady hand, and
bound him, and laid him on the wood upon the
altar.   And did not his resolution now fail?
Did he not now say or feel that he could not
perform the fatal act?   No.   His purpose to
obey was fixed.   "He stretched forth his hand,
and took the knife to slay his son."   O what a
time was that!   Another moment, and Isaac
would have been a bleeding, dying victim on
the altar.   But this was the moment for God
to prevent the fatal deed.   The voice said,
"Abraham, Abraham, lay not thine hand upon
the lad; for now I know that thou fearest God,

seeing thou hast not withheld thy son, thine
only son from me." And Abraham looked and
saw that God had indeed *provided himself a
lamb* for the burnt-offering. A ram, caught in
a thicket by his horns, supplied the place of
Isaac, and bled and was burnt upon the altar.

Now the trial was over; and God knew, and
all men knew, that Abraham feared the Lord
and would obey him. His faith was now fully
proved, and his example would always remain to
teach others what faith is, and to show that it is
always best for them to trust in God and obey
him. God will always take care of those who
believe what he says, and do what he commands. The example of Abraham is proof of it.

With what gratitude and gladness now could
this father and son return to their own dwelling-place. How joyful their hearts, as they
travelled on the way, in thinking and speaking
of this new proof of the divine favor, and of
the certainty that all the promises of God to
them, and their seed after them, would be fulfilled. But before they left the place of their
trial and their joy, Abraham gave it a new
name: "he called the name of the place
Jehovah-Jireh," which here means, "the Lord

will provide." This is a most precious truth. Abraham doubtless believed it before; and it may be that he did not need, on his own account, this new and trying proof of it. But others in all ages needed it, and many have been encouraged by this example to trust the Lord.

And this is the use which I wish all my young readers to make of this example. I want you to remember how the Lord provided for Abraham, because he believed the Lord's words and obeyed the Lord's commands. And if you will believe and obey what God tells you in the Bible, he will provide for you. Think how Abraham left his country and his father's house, and became a stranger in a strange land, and the Lord blessed him. And then think that the Saviour tells *you*, that if you will deny yourself and follow him, if you will forsake father and mother, and houses and lands, and be his disciple, he will bless you, and you shall be happy. Abraham believed and obeyed, and obtained the blessing. Will *you* believe and obey, and obtain the blessing? Do you not need the favor of God? Do you not need pardon and salvation? Then seek these blessings by believing what God says, and doing what he commands.

Think also how God provided for Abraham when he was about to sacrifice his son. You may never want him to provide for you in just such a manner ; but you do want him to provide for you the way of escape from sin and hell—you do need his blessing to bring you to happiness and heaven. Will you not then believe and obey God? This is the only way to obtain his blessing.

When all the world was in a state of sin and danger, when we were all exposed to a worse death than Isaac was about to suffer, God provided a Lamb to suffer in our stead. "Christ died for our sins, and not for ours only, but for the sins of the whole world." The whole human race being sinners against God, were exposed to the pains of *eternal death*, that is, we were in danger of endless misery. Then, the Scripture says, " God so loved the world that he gave his only begotten Son, that whosoever believeth in him should not perish, but have everlasting life." When the Saviour came into the world, John the Baptist, pointing to him, said, "Behold the *Lamb* of God."

Jesus, then, is the Lamb whom God has provided for *us* in our state of sin and danger. He has suffered and died for us. He has been slain in your stead, for your sake, my young reader. Now if you would be saved from sin and hell, you must *believe* in him. The example of Abraham shows you what it is to believe. When God spake to Abraham, he believed what God said, and did what God commanded. God speaks to you in the Bible; he tells you that he sent his Son to save you, that Jesus died for your sins, and that if you will trust in this Saviour, and be his disciple, you shall be saved. Now *you must believe what God says in such a manner that you will do what he commands.* That is believing; that would make you like Abraham; it would be true faith.

And now, my young reader, will you not thus believe? God requires you to do it. You ought to do it. You can do it, if you will. Why then should you not do it? As God has sent his Son to be sacrificed as a lamb for you, it is your duty to believe and be saved. If you will not believe and obey God, you must perish; and you will deserve to perish.

CHAPTER V.

MOSES.

THE interesting story of the birth of MOSES, and of his being hid three months to keep him from the hands of the cruel Pharoah, and of his being put by his mother into a little ark of bulrushes and laid on the bank of the river, and of his being taken up by Pharoah's daughter, you can read in the second chapter of Exodus. I cannot, in this little book, speak of these things, though it would be pleasing to do so. I must begin with Moses when he became a man, and when he began to do those things which made him so remarkable, and which showed his faith.

In this case, also, I will begin with what the apostle says about him in Heb. 11. " By faith Moses, when he was come to years, refused to be called the son of Pharoah's daughter ; choosing rather to suffer affliction with the people of God, than to enjoy the pleasures of sin for a season ; esteeming the reproach of Christ greater riches than the treasures of Egypt : for he had respect unto the recompense of the reward." Here is an example of faith, showing itself in a different manner from any we have before noticed. Moses was a great man in Egypt. The king's daughter, who had taken him when he was an infant from the river's brink, had adopted him as her own son. He was, therefore, a prince; and perhaps he would have been king, had he remained in the family of Pharoah till the old king died. The words of the apostle, where he says that Moses esteemed "the reproach of Christ greater riches than the treasures of Egypt," seem to imply that the treasures of Egypt might have been his, if he had not left them. In countries where kings rule with absolute power, as they did in Egypt, the treasures of the nation belong to the king. But whether Moses would have been king or not, had he stayed in Egypt, it is plain that he had, while he remained in the king's family, riches and honors in abundance. He had all those things which men of worldly feelings esteem so highly. He had honors, for he was a prince in a splendid court and mighty kingdom. He had power, for he was the adopted son of the king's daughter, and probably the heir to the throne. He had riches, for the treasures of Egypt were his. He had knowledge, for the Scripture says, "He was learned in all the wisdom of the Egyptians, and was mighty in words and in deeds." Acts 7 : 22. In regard to worldly things, what could he have more? He had all that his heart could wish.

Most men would think, if they could be in such a situation as Moses was, if they could have all that he had, and enjoy all that he enjoyed in worldly things, they should be happy. Perhaps you, my young reader, have thought, if you had a great and splendid house, rich furniture and food, an elegant carriage and horses, and plenty of money, you would be happy, and want nothing more. But these things would never make you happy. They never made any man happy. A man must have something better than all these things, or he will never enjoy true happiness. He must have a heart to love God and obey him; he must have faith in God and do his commandments, or he will never find true happiness in this world, or the world to come.

So Moses thought. He knew that his wealth and honors could never satisfy the desires of his immortal soul, and therefore he sought his pleasures in serving God. He knew that this world and all things in it would be destroyed, and therefore he sought a better world, and laid up his treasures in heaven. He knew that it was dangerous to be delighted with worldly riches and honors, and therefore he " chose rather to suffer affliction with the people of God, than to enjoy the pleasures of sin for a season." It was his belief of what God said, that made him choose a portion in heaven, rather than a portion on earth. It was his *faith*, his trust in God, his firm belief that God would take care of him, and make him happy, if he would obey him and do his duty—it was this which made Moses willing to forsake the treasures and the throne of Egypt, and go and join himself to a poor and despised people.

Moses' brethren, the children of Israel, were slaves in the land of Egypt. You remember the story of Joseph being sold into Egypt, and of his brethren and his father going to dwell there when there was a famine in the land of Canaan. You remember how Joseph provided for them, and gave them a place to dwell in

the best of the land. Though they were few
in number when they first went down into
Egypt, yet they afterwards greatly increased,
so that they became a very numerous people.
And after Joseph and his father and his brothers died, the Egyptians began to oppress the
children of Israel. They made slaves of them.
Moses was one of the children of Israel, though
he had been brought up in Pharoah's house.
He saw the oppressions of his brethren. He
knew how cruelly they were treated, and he
was grieved with their afflictions.

But this people, though they were in bondage, and in much oppression, were the chosen
people of God. They were the posterity of
Abraham, and God had promised to them the
land of Canaan as their dwelling-place. All
this Moses knew, and he resolved to unite himself with his brethren, though they were poor
and despised, and to try to make their condition better. He forsook the palace of the
king, to dwell in the cottages of the poor. He
left the company of the gay and the great, to
become the companion of the sorrowful and the
oppressed. He forsook the ease and the treasures of Egypt, to endure the toil of forty years'

wandering in the wilderness, and to be fed with manna from heaven. This showed his faith. He believed that God had spoken good concerning Israel, and therefore was willing to unite his interests with that poor and despised people. He believed that God would fulfil his promises to the seed of Abraham and Isaac and Jacob, and therefore he led his brethren forth out of the land of Egypt, relying entirely for food and protection on the providence of God. He believed that the children of Israel would at length find a resting-place in Canaan, "a land flowing with milk and honey;" and though he never entered that land himself, and only saw it afar off, yet, during forty years' wandering, he never doubted the word of the Lord, but with the eye of faith looked forward, and saw his brethren quietly settled in the land of promise. This was faith. It was relying firmly on what God had said, and acting accordingly. This is the kind of faith which God requires, and which the Bible teaches.

In this world, where men in general are so selfish and worldly-minded, we find but few who are willing to give up great earthly enjoyments and prospects, for the sake of de-

MOSES.   65

voting themselves to the service of God. Most
persons seek their portion in this world, and
neglect the things of eternity. They choose
to have their good things in their lifetime, like
the rich man mentioned by the Saviour in the
parable. Not so with Moses. He, as the
apostle says, "had respect unto the recompense of the reward." He looked not for present ease, but for future happiness. He fully
believed that he should have more peace of
mind, and more true happiness, even in this
world, if he united himself with God's people,
and shared in their labors and sacrifices, than
he should have in all the riches and pleasures
of Egypt. And he believed, too, that if he
denied himself and served God, he should have
a dwelling-place in heaven; and this would be
a "recompense of reward" infinitely richer
than all the joys and treasures of earth. This
made him willing to "suffer affliction with the
people of God, rather than to enjoy the pleasures of sin for a season." He well knew that
if he left the palace of Pharoah, and joined
himself with his brethren in bondage, he must
have many trials, would be persecuted by the
king, and despised by his former companions,

would have a life of toil, and that his rest must be sought beyond the grave. But though he knew these things, he did not hesitate. As the Scripture says, "he esteemed the reproach of Christ greater riches than the treasures of Egypt." That is, he had rather be reproach- ed for his religion than to be flattered for his greatness. He had rather be despised by wicked men for his piety, than to be admired for his riches. He had rather be poor on earth, and have a title to a heavenly kingdom, than to have Egypt's throne, and fail of obtaining everlasting life.

Now I want my young reader should get much benefit from this example of Moses. I want you to believe, as Moses did, that there are better things than any which this world affords. I want you to believe fully, that a treasure in heaven is worth far more than all the treasures of the world. If you do truly and with all your heart believe this, you will be much more anxious to be a disciple of Jesus Christ, and to love and serve God, than you are to gain the riches and honors of this world What can wealth or worldly honor profit you, when you are on your sick and dying bed?

But if at that hour you have an interest in the Saviour, you will have the *true riches*, and be happy for ever.

I want you to believe, as Moses did, that it is better for you to be united with the people of God, than to enjoy the pleasures of sin; and that it is better even to suffer affliction with Christians, than to be flattered by wicked men, and unite with their company. It is true, that at the present day pious people are not so much persecuted and afflicted as they were in former times, and we ought to be thankful to God for this. But even now, in this Christian land, true believers are often reproached on account of their religion. And many young persons are afraid to be serious, and to seek the salvation of their souls, because they think that their careless companions will reproach and laugh at them. Cast away such fears as these. Remember, Moses esteemed reproach for Christ's sake greater riches than the treasures of Egypt. Let his example cheer you. If you do your duty and embrace the Saviour, God will take care of you; he will be your friend, and his friendship is worth more than all the praises of men.

I want you to believe, as Moses did, that God speaks to you, and that in the Bible he tells you what to do. For he does speak to you in his holy word, as truly as he spoke unto Moses in the burning bush. He speaks to you in a different manner; but it is none the less real. God speaks in the Bible. He speaks to *you*. Believe this, and believe also that it is altogether best that you should obey him, and do as he commands you to do. If you honestly believe thus, and *act* as if you believed it, you will have true faith. Such is the faith that pleases God, that makes a Christian, and that saves the soul.

This is the faith, my young reader, which I want you to have. And why should you not have it? Will you not believe God? Does he not speak truly? Does he not speak to you? Why then should you not believe him? And why should you not believe in such a manner that you will do what God commands you?

Read, study, and think about what God has told you in the Bible respecting a Saviour. Jesus came to save you. But if you would be saved by him, you must believe in him. And

is he not just such a Saviour as you need?
You are a sinner, and there is no other Saviour
for sinners. Will you not then accept of him?
Will you not believe what is said about him in
the Bible? Will you not trust yourself in his
hands? It is safe to trust in him, and there
is safety nowhere else. "Believe on the Lord
Jesus Christ, and thou shalt be saved." So
God tells you in the holy Scriptures. But
your belief must be of that kind which will
lead you to obey God, and to do the commandments of Jesus Christ. Never be contented
without such a belief. The salvation of your
soul depends on it. For "he that believeth
and is baptized shall be saved; but he that
believeth not, shall be damned."

CHAPTER VI.

DANIEL AND HIS THREE FRIENDS.

THE examples contained·in the former chapters have showed what faith is, and how it is manifested in the conduct of good men who believed the word of God, and did what he commanded them to do. In this chapter, I propose to set before my young readers some examples in which faith was exhibited by pious men who refused to do what God had forbidden. They would not .obey the commands of men, when those commands were contrary to the word of God. There is no difference in the *faith*, it is the same principle in both cases. But there is some difference in the manner of showing it, and this will render it useful to look at some examples of this kind.

The Bible gives us many such examples; but as I cannot mention them all, I .have chosen to speak of DANIEL AND HIS THREE FRIENDS. The example of these persons, even when they were children, as well as when they became men, will show what faith is, by

showing their steady resolution not to disobey
God in order to please men.

In the first chapter of the book of Daniel,
we read that Nebuchadnezzar king of Babylon
came and besieged Jerusalem, and took the
city, and made captive the king of Judah and
his people, and carried them and many of the
vessels of the temple into Babylon. At that
time the men of Judah were, in general, very
wicked in the sight of God, and God gave
them into the hands of their enemies. They
were taken prisoners and carried into captivity
in a far country. But though most of them
were very sinful, and had offended God by
their wicked doings, yet there were a few who
feared God and obeyed his commandments.
Among these were four children, who appear
to have been pious in their childhood. Their
names were Daniel, Hananiah, Mishael, and
Azariah.

After the captives had arrived at Babylon,
Nebuchadnezzar the king ordered one of his
officers to choose out from among the children
some of the most active and intelligent and
best looking, that they might be taught the
language and learning of Babylon, and might

be prepared to live in the king's palace. This officer chose out a large number, and among them were Daniel and his three friends. We do not know the ages of these children; perhaps they were from eight to fourteen or sixteen years old. "And the king appointed them a daily provision of the king's meat, and of the wine which he drank; so nourishing them three years, that at the end thereof they might stand before the king. But Daniel purposed in his heart, that he would not defile himself with the portion of the king's meat, nor with the wine which he drank." Here we have the singular example of a youth who refused to obey a king's command, because he thought that command was contrary to the law of God. He would not do wrong, even when the king commanded him to do it. With him, also, Hananiah, Mishael, and Azariah united, and they all refused to defile themselves with the portion which the king provided for them. They understood that the law of God forbade them to partake of such things, and they refused to do it. This refusal, it may be, put their lives in danger. If the king had heard of it, he would probably have been angry, and

might

might have ordered them to be killed. But this danger did not make them willing to disobey God. They resolved to do what God said, not what the king said, and risk the consequences. In this they showed their faith. They believed God's word, and were willing to trust themselves in his care. This is faith.

And God did take care of them. Though they lived on pulse and water, yet "their countenances appeared fairer and fatter in flesh than all the children which did eat the portion of the king's meat." And when they all came to stand before the king, at the end of three years, "the king communed with them; and among them all was none found like Daniel, Hananiah, Mishael, and Azariah: therefore they stood before the king." He took them into his palace, and they became his counsellors. He showed much regard for them, and gave them many honors.

As they feared God in their childhood, they continued to fear him in their manhood. This might be expected. As in their youth they believed God's word, obeyed his commands, and trusted in his care, we might suppose that, when they were older, they would show

the same example of faith. If they would not
when young disobey God to please the king,
neither would they do it when they were old.
They all had the trial afterwards, and their
faith did not fail.

The first trial came on Hananiah, Mishael,
and Azariah. The names of these three, given
them by the man who had the care of them
before they were presented to the king, were
Shadrach, Meshach, and Abed-nego. By these
names they were afterwards called. You may
find the account of their great trial in the third
chapter of the book of Daniel. It was in this
manner.

"Nebuchadnezzar the king made an image
of gold, whose height was threescore cubits,
and the breadth thereof six cubits. He set it
up in the plain of Dura, in the province of
Babylon." This image he called a god, and
he made it in order to worship it. This was
contrary to the law of God, for God had said in
one of the ten commandments, "Thou shalt
not make unto thee any graven image, or any
likeness of any thing that is in heaven above,
or that is in the earth beneath, or that is in the
waters under the earth. Thou shalt not bow

down thyself to them nor serve them; for I
the Lord thy God am a jealous God, visiting
the iniquity of the fathers upon the children,
unto the third and fourth generation of them
that hate me; and showing mercy unto thousands of them that love me and keep my commandments." The command of God, therefore, strictly forbids the making and worship-
ping of images. But Nebuchadnezzar made
the image, and said that all the people in his
kingdom should worship it. He called together
a great multitude of the chief men of his kingdom, and gave the command in this manner:
" To you it is commanded, O people, nations,
and languages, that at what time ye hear the
sound of the cornet, flute, harp, sackbut, psal-
tery, dulcimer, and all kinds of music, ye fall
down and worship the golden image that Nebuchadnezzar the king has set up; and whoso
falleth not down and worshippeth, shall the
same hour be cast into the midst of a burning
fiery furnace." So when the music sounded,
the whole multitude fell down and worshipped
the image, except Shadrach, Meshach, and
Abed-nego.

These three men would not worship the

image. Where Daniel was at this time, we
are not told; but we may be sure that if he
had been present, he would have united with
his friends, and would have done as they did.
They believed that God had commanded them
not to worship images, and they resolved to
obey God rather than man. They trusted that
God would take care of them. But whatever
should happen to them, they determined that
they would not do wrong to please the king or
any body else. Here was faith, strong faith.
They believed God's word, trusted in him, and
did their duty.

The king was exceedingly angry when he
found that they had disobeyed him. He called
them before him in great wrath, and told them
he would give them another chance to worship
the image, if they would do it, when the music
sounded again; and if they would not do it, he
told them that they should be cast into the
burning fiery furnace. They said to the king,
" We are not careful to answer thee in this
matter. If it be so, our God whom we serve
is able to deliver us from the burning fiery
furnace, and he will deliver us out of thy hand,
O king. But if not, be it known unto thee, O

king, *that we will not serve thy gods, nor worship the golden image which thou hast set up.*"
This answer so enraged the king, that in the fury of his anger he ordered the furnace to be heated "one seven times more than it was wont to be heated," and then he commanded the strongest men in his army to bind Shadrach, Meshach, and Abed-nego, and cast them into the furnace. They did it; "and these three men fell down bound into the midst of the burning fiery furnace."

And were not these men immediately consumed by the flames? No. God preserved them. They trusted in God, they believed that he was able to deliver them. Their faith pleased God, and he did deliver them. One from heaven was with them, and they received no harm. The astonished king looked into the furnace, and said, "Lo, I see four men loose, walking in the midst of the fire, and they have no hurt; and the form of the fourth is like the Son of God." He was then convinced that the golden image which he had made was nothing, that idol worship was folly, and that there was no God but the true God. He came near to the mouth of the furnace, and said,

"Shadrach, Meshach, and Abed-nego, ye servants of the most high God, come forth, and come hither." Then these men came forth, and it was found that the fire had no power over them. They were safe, for their God preserved them.

Behold in this example, my young reader, what faith is, and what are its fruits. See how those three men believed God's word and trusted in him, and were delivered. They believed that God had told them not to worship an idol, and they would not disobey God because a man commanded them to do it. Though they knew that they should be cast into the fire, yet this did not make them willing to sin. They would not do a wicked act to avoid the flames. God was pleased with their faith and their conduct, and he helped and saved them.

Learn from this to trust in God. Remember, that it will always be best for you to obey God, and not do wrong to please men. If others do wrong, and wish you to do likewise, refuse, and say you will not do wickedly and sin against God.

We will now take a view of the conduct of

DANIEL, when he was put on a severe trial of
his faith. This was long after the trial of his
three friends, and another king ruled in Babylon. This king, whose name was Darius,
made Daniel, next to himself, the first ruler in
the kingdom. The account you may read in
the sixth chapter of Daniel. "It pleased Darius to set over the kingdom an hundred and
twenty princes, which should be over the whole
kingdom, and over these, three presidents, of
whom Daniel was first." He was made first
because he was best. He was a good and
pious man, and "an excellent spirit was found
in him."

But the other presidents and princes did not
like Daniel. They envied him because he was
raised above them. They hated his religion,
for he worshipped the true God, and they worshipped idols. They could not bear to have his
bright example shining on their wicked habits.
They therefore resolved to find some cause of
complaint which they might present to the
king against him, and so have him destroyed.
But Daniel's conduct in all the affairs of the
government was so good, that they could not
find any accusation against him. He did his

duty to the king and to the people so well, that
they could find no cause of complaint.   Then
they said among themselves, " We shall not
find any occasion against this Daniel, except
we find it against him concerning the law of
his God."   What a proof was this of his goodness, when even his enemies could find nothing
against him, unless they made his religion a
cause of complaint.   They knew that he prayed daily to his God, and they thought he would
be unwilling to omit praying.   In view of this
habit of prayer, they laid a plan to procure his
destruction.

They went to the king and urged him to
sign a decree that no man should pray for
thirty days.   The king did not know for what
purpose they wished him to make such a law.
He did not suspect that they were laying a
plan to destroy the best man in the kingdom.
So he signed the decree, which said no man
should make a petition to any God or man,
except to the king, for thirty days.   As soon
as this decree was signed, it could not be
changed, for the laws of the Medes and Per-
sians altered not.   Any one who should pray
during these thirty days, would be cast into

the den of lions. The man who should offer a prayer to God must die.

What did Daniel do? Did he continue to pray? He knew that one prayer would expose him to death. He knew that the law was made by his enemies to ensnare and ruin him. And he knew that they would watch him, and would not fail to accuse him, if he should continue his habit of praying to God. But all this did not alarm him. He resolved to attend to his own duty and leave the consequences with God. It was his duty, he believed, to pray daily. God had commanded this, and he thought that no king or set of men had any right to forbid it. Therefore he determined to obey God rather than man. And the Bible says, "When Daniel knew that the writing was signed, he went into his house; and his windows being open in his chamber towards Jerusalem, he kneeled upon his knees three times a day, and prayed and gave thanks before his God, as he did aforetime." When he did this, he knew that he must be cast into the den of lions; but he would not omit his duty to avoid the jaws of lions. He would not do wrong to save his life. He believed that God was able to deliver him from the power of the lions; and if he was not delivered, he believed that God would make him happy after death. He trusted in God, and did his duty. This was faith, and it was showing his faith to all men.

His enemies accused him to the king, and Daniel was cast into the lion's den. But the Lord preserved him. He remained in the den all night, but the lions did not hurt him. When the morning came, and the king called unto Daniel, he answered, "My God hath sent his angel, and hath shut the lions' mouths, that they have not hurt me." The king was glad, and he commanded that Daniel should be taken up out of the den; and then he commanded his accusers to be thrown in. As soon as these enemies of Daniel fell into the den, the lions tore them to pieces.

Thus was Daniel preserved because he had faith, because he believed God's word, and did his own duty. He would not neglect to pray because a king's decree commanded him not to pray. He would not disobey God at a man's bidding, and God took care of him. So will God take care of every man who does his duty, and will not be turned aside from the path of obedience. There is no promise that God will always preserve the *lives* of those who are in danger of death by their obedience. But he has promised to make all things work together for their good, whether life or death. He has promised to be with them in trouble, to give them peace and joy in believing, and to take them to heaven.

From the example of Daniel and his three friends, my young reader may learn many important things. You may learn what it is to believe God and trust in him. You may learn that it is always best to do what God commands, and leave the event with him. And you may also learn to refuse to do wrong, when others urge you to do so. Never do a wicked thing to please others. You may sometimes be with those who use wicked language, tell lies, violate the Sabbath, or steal, and they may wish you to do as they do. Perhaps they may laugh at you, if you refuse to be as wicked as they are. At such times remember how Daniel and his friends acted. Do as they did. Refuse to do wrong. Whoever urges you, say that you will not do a wicked thing, and sin against God. It would be better for you to bear the reproaches of the wicked, than to be like them. It would be better for you to die, than to pursue a wicked course of life, and go down to eternal misery.

CONCLUSION.

My young reader, have you read this book thus far attentively? Can you remember what has been said about the faith of Abel, and Enoch, and Noah, and Abraham, and Moses, and Daniel and his three friends? And do you remember, too, how Mr. Cecil taught his little daughter what faith is, and how she threw her beads into the fire, trusting in her father that it would be best for her to do so? And do you also remember what I told you about your going to find the money under the stone, if your father should tell you that there was such a treasure and where you might find it? If you have read with attention, and remember what you have read, you will always understand the nature of faith. If any one should ask you, What is faith? you can answer, that it is *believing the truth;* it is a *belief of what God says;* and it is that kind of belief which makes a person *act* as if he believed. If any one should ask you, What is *Christian* faith, or the faith by which a sinner is justified? you can say, *It is that state of*

mind in which a sinner, humbled and penitent,
looks to Christ alone for salvation, trusting
in him, loving him, and obeying him.

Now you need never forget this. It is so
simple that you may always remember it.
Many have supposed that it is very difficult to
understand what faith is. And it must be
owned, that many things have been said and
written about it which have tended to make
it dark, and hard to be understood. But there
is no need of this. Faith is very simple.
Even a child may understand it ; and what is
better, a child may *have* it. You need not
wait till you are fifteen or twenty years old
before you believe. If you are able to read
and understand this book, you may exercise
faith now. Many children six, eight, or ten
years old, have had that faith which saved their
souls, and gave them a title to heaven.

How old are you, my young reader? Are
you six, eight, ten, twelve, or fifteen years
old? You are old enough, then, to believe in
Christ to the saving of your soul. You know
what the Bible says about the Saviour. You
know what the Saviour said about the wretched state of sinners. You know that Jesus

came to seek and to save them which were lost; that he pointed out the way that leads to heaven; that he invited all men to become his friends, to deny themselves, and take up the cross and follow him. You know that Jesus spoke of the day of judgment, of heaven and hell, and that he promised to save all who would be his disciples, and obey his commandments. You know that he said, "He that believeth and is baptized, shall be saved; but he that believeth not, shall be damned." And you know also, that Jesus "gave his life a ransom for many;" that he died a cruel death on the cross to save sinners. Now this is enough for you to know in order to exercise faith, and be saved. If you believe these things truly, if you will believe them so that you will *act* as if you believed them, that will be *saving faith.* And can you not thus believe? Will you not?

You may remember that it was said, in the former part of this book, that the great object of the Christian's faith is the Lord Jesus Christ. He is the only Saviour of them that believe; and it is their faith in him which is the condition of their pardon and their eternal happiness. The real Christian, it is true, believes many other things besides those which are said about the Saviour. He believes all that God has said in the Bible. He receives the whole of that blessed book as the word of God. But it is his belief in Christ which *saves* him. This is "the only name given under heaven among men, whereby we must be saved." There is no other way of salvation. The good men whom I have mentioned in this book, and who lived before the Son of God dwelt on earth, believed in a Saviour to come. Abel and Enoch and Abraham and others believed in One who was to come after they lived, even in that great Prophet, Jesus Christ, whom the Lord promised to raise up for his people. Jesus said, "Abraham rejoiced to see my day; and he saw it, and was glad." Now, all pious men believe in the Saviour who has come. And it is this belief which secures their salvation; as the Scripture says, "Believe on the Lord Jesus Christ, and thou shalt be saved."

The same state of mind, however, which believes the word of God in respect to one thing, will believe the word of God in respect to any other thing. The man who believes what God has said in the Old Testament, will also believe what he has said in the New Testament. If you believe the testimony of God respecting David, you will also believe his testimony respecting his Son Jesus Christ. So that if you have faith in one thing that God has spoken, you will have faith in all things that God has spoken. This shows you that faith is always the same in all ages of the world. The faith of Abel was like the faith of any good man at the present day. And though Abel lived long before the Saviour came into the world, yet, if he lived now, he would, with the same state of mind he then had, be a believer in the Lord Jesus Christ.

And I wish you, my young reader, to be a true believer in the Lord Jesus Christ. I have written this little book to persuade you to believe. It has been my object, not only to show you what faith is, but to urge you to exercise it. And will you not believe in Christ? Think of what he has said and done and suffered for you. Think of his good instructions and kind invitations. Think of his warnings and threatenings. Think how "God so loved the world, that he gave his only begotten Son, that whosoever believeth in him should not perish, but have everlasting life." And now, will you not believe? Has not the Saviour done enough to convince you that you ought to trust yourself in his hands, and become his disciple? What more could he have done for you than he has done? Has he not died for you? And can you now refuse to hear his voice? Will you not be his friend and follower? Will you not believe in him, trust in him; that is, will you not have *faith* in him?

Remember, I pray you, why you need faith. Being a sinner, you must have it, or perish. You have in a thousand ways transgressed the laws of God, and you deserve the penalty of those laws, which is eternal misery. And there is no way for you to escape this dreadful doom, but by faith in Christ. O think of this seriously and earnestly. Consider how guilty sin has made you in the sight of God. Reflect not only on your outward transgressions, but on the depravity of your heart, on the evil passions and wicked thoughts and feelings which have lodged in your bosom. All these are offensive to God, and deserve his wrath.

And there is no way for you to escape that wrath and obtain forgiveness but by faith in Jesus Christ. He offers to pardon you, if you will exercise faith in him, and rely on his atoning sacrifice for your justification. O then go to him, cast yourself at his feet, trust in what he has done to save you, and give yourself to his service. *This will be faith.* And all who have such faith will be saved.

But do you say, that faith " is the gift of God," and that you cannot have it unless he bestows it upon you ? I know it is so—the Bible declares it. But if you feel your *need* of faith, will you not ask for it ? If you feel that you shall perish without it, will you not pray earnestly to God that he will give it—that he will help you to believe on his Son ? If you feel that you are sinking under the weight of your sins, will you not cry to the Saviour, as Peter did when sinking in the sea, " Lord, save me, or I perish ?" Certainly you will. It is true that faith is the gift of God ; but he does not give it to careless, thoughtless minds. He bestows it on those who feel that they are lost, and shall perish without it. He imparts it to those who inquire anxiously, " What must we do to be saved?" And this is the state of mind which I wish all the readers of this little book to have. When you feel this, when you are deeply convinced of sin, when you tremble in view of your guilt and danger, you will cry to God for help. You will ask him to enable you to exercise that faith in Christ which will secure your pardon and salvation.

O that you might *now* feel this need. As you finish reading this book, O say in your heart, "I must have true faith in Christ, or perish. I will ask God to give me this faith. I will arise and go to my Father, and say to him, O help me to believe in Christ, that my soul may be saved, and that I may love and serve thee for ever."

Now, my young reader, I must take my leave of you. May this little book do you good. I pray that you may be a true believer in Jesus Christ; and I hope that you and I shall meet together in heaven.

SGCB Titles for the Young

Solid Ground Christian Books is honored to be able to offer over a dozen uncovered treasure for children and young people.

The Safe Compass and How it Points by Richard Newton is another gem from the heart of "the Prince of preachers to the young," according to Charles Haddon Spurgeon.

Bible Warnings: *Sermons to Children on Dangers that lie along their Path and How to Avoid Them* by Richard Newton is the sequel to *Bible Promises* that you hold in your hand. Fifteen brilliant chapters..

Bible Promises: *Sermons to Children on God's Word as our Solid Rock* by Richard Newton directs children to rest in the certain promises of God.

Heroes of the Reformation by Richard Newton is a unique volume that introduces children and young people to the leading figures and incidents of the Reformation.

Heroes of the Early Church by Richard Newton is the sequel to the above-named volume. The very last book Newton wrote introduces all the leading figures of the early church with lessons to be learned from each figure.

The King's Highway: *Ten Commandments to the Young* by Richard Newton is a volume of Newton's sermons to children. Highly recommended!

The Life of Jesus Christ for the Young by Richard Newton is a double volume set that traces the Gospel from Genesis 3:15 to the Ascension of our Lord and the outpouring of His Spirit on the Day of Pentecost. Excellent!

The Child's Book on the Fall by Thomas H. Gallaudet is a simple and practical exposition of the Fall of man into sin, and his only hope of salvation.

The Child's Book on Repentance by Thomas H. Gallaudet is a simple and practical exposition of the Fall of man into sin, and his only hope of salvation.

The Child's Book on the Soul by Thomas H. Gallaudet is a simple and practical exposition of the Fall of man into sin, and his only hope of salvation.

The Child's Book on the Sabbath by Horace Hooker is written in the same style as those of his dear friend T.H. Gallaudet (see above titles). Instruction is given, objections answered with wisdom and grace.

The Child at Home by John S.C. Abbott is the sequel to his popular book *The Mother at Home*. A must read for children and their parents.

My Brother's Keeper: *Letters to a Younger Brother* by J.W. Alexander contains the actual letters Alexander sent to his ten year old brother.

The Scripture Guide by J.W. Alexander is filled with page after page of information on getting the most from our Bibles. Invaluable!

Feed My Lambs: *Lectures to Children* by John Todd is drawn from actual sermons preached in Philadelphia, PA and Pittsfield, MA to the children of the church, one Sunday each month. A pure goldmine of instruction.

Truth Made Simple: *The Attributes of God for Children* by John Todd was intended to be a miniature Systematic Theology for children. Richard Newton said that Dr. Todd taught him how to teach children. Practical and crystal clear!

The Young Lady's Guide by Harvey Newcomb will speak directly to the heart of the young women who desire to serve Christ with all their being.

The Chief End of Man by John Hall is an exposition and application of the first question of the Westminster Shorter Catechism. Full of rich illustrations.

Call us Toll Free at 1-877-666-9469
Send us an e-mail at sgcb@charter.net
Visit us on line at solid-ground-books.com

CPSIA information can be obtained at www.ICGtesting.com
Printed in the USA
LVOW06s0536211213

366091LV00002B/152/A

9 781599 250649